Platonic Scripts

DONALD JUSTICE

Ann Arbor
The University of Michigan Press

1987   1986   1985   1984   4   3   2   1

Library of Congress Cataloging in Publication Data

Justice, Donald Rodney, 1925–
    Platonic scripts.

    (Poets on poetry)
    1. Justice, Donald Rodney, 1925–   —Interviews.
    2. Poets, American—20th century—Interviews.
    3. Poetry—Addresses, essays, lectures.   I. Title.
    II. Series.
    PS3519.U825P5   1984   818'.5408   84-7215
    ISBN 0-472-06352-9 (pbk.)

For Henri Coulette

"Mountains are again Mountains"

Acknowledgments

Grateful acknowledgment is made to the following journals, publishers, and institutions for permission to reprint copyrighted material.

Antaeus for "Meters and Memory," *Antaeus* nos. 30–31 (Spring 1978). Also for "The Free-Verse Line in Stevens," *Antaeus* no. 53 (Fall 1984). Copyright © 1978, 1984 by *Antaeus*. Reprinted by permission.

Avon Books for "Notes on 'Variations on Southern Themes.'" From *Singular Voices*, edited by Stephen Berg. Copyright © 1984.

Field for "On Purity of Style," *Field* no. 29 (Fall 1983).

Iowa Council of Teachers of English and the English Department of the University of Iowa for "The Private History of a Poem" (formerly "The History of 'Anonymous Drawing'"), *Iowa English Yearbook*, Fall 1961.

The Iowa Review for an interview with David Hamilton and Lowell Edwin Folsom, *The Iowa Review* 11, nos. 2–3 (Spring–Summer 1980). Also for "Notes of an Outsider," *The Iowa Review* 13, nos. 3–4 (1984). Copyright © 1980, 1984 by *The Iowa Review*.

Longman for "On Writing 'First Death'," from *Fifty Contemporary Poets: The Creative Process*, edited by Alberta T. Turner. Also for "Bus Stop: Or, Fear and Loneliness on Potrero Hill," from *Fifty-One Contemporary Poets*, edited by Alberta T. Turner. Copyright © 1977, 1984 by Longman Inc. Reprinted by permission of Longman Inc., New York.

Mankato State University *Muse* (a successor to *Plaintiff*) for an interview with Cynthia Lofsness and Kathy Otto, *Plaintiff*, Spring 1966.

The Missouri Review for an interview with Larry Levis, *The Missouri Review* 4, no. 1 (Fall 1980).

The New Yorker for "In the Train, Heading North Through Florida." Reprinted by permission; © 1983 Donald Justice. Originally published in *The New Yorker*.

The Ohio Review for an interview with Wayne Dodd and Stanley Plumly, originally titled "Effacement of the Self," *The Ohio Review* 16, no. 3 (Spring 1975).

The Prairie Schooner for an interview with Gregory Fitz Gerald and William Heyen, *The Prairie Schooner* 47, no. 4 (Winter 1973–74). Copyright © 1974 by the University of Nebraska Press.

Seneca Review for an interview with Geoffrey Clark, Robert Crotty, and Robert L. McRoberts, *Seneca Review* 2, no. 1 (April 1971).

The Texas Review (formerly *The Sam Houston Literary Review*) for an interview with Paul Ruffin, *The Sam Houston Literary Review* 3, no. 1 (April 1978).

University of Texas Press for "Baudelaire: The Question of His Sincerity," *The Texas Quarterly* 1, no. 1 (February 1958).

Every effort has been made to trace the ownership of all copyrighted material and to secure permission for its use.

Contents

Preface

Of all the poets of my generation who did not get much into the habit of criticism—and that would include the great majority of us—I may be the only one with any regrets at having kept my thoughts more or less to myself. I see now that criticism can be of enormous value in helping to define and refine one's own thinking; and there is always the chance, if it is any good, that it might do the same for another's.

In revising the interviews I have tried not to compromise the spontaneity and conversational flow which are the seasoning of this highly perishable form. Otherwise I felt free to improve the prose of my remarks a little, to cut out some of the inevitable overlappings between interviews, and even to suppress a few opinions which embarrassed me the second time around. The middle section—"Notes of an Outsider"—was put together out of scribbled loose pages, paragraphs from lectures, and an earnest notebook kept very sporadically.

Donald Justice
Gainesville, Florida
September 1983

I

Interviews

An Interview with
Cynthia Lofsness and Kathy Otto

(The following interview took place in the home of Marvin Bell. It was near dusk. The children were getting restless. Mr. Justice's young son, who was playing in the yard with Nathan Bell, occasionally came into the room to remind his father it was getting close to supper time. Mr. Justice assured him they were going to join George Starbuck and his children for supper. Mr. Bell and some friends who were visiting him were chattering in the kitchen and aside from an occasional telephone call we proceeded fairly smoothly throughout most of the interview, which ended rather abruptly as we ran out of tape.)

Shall we start at the beginning?

What do you mean?

Where you were born, where you went to school, traveled, and so on.

I was born in Miami, Florida, and went to school there through most of my undergraduate work. M.A. at Chapel Hill. A year at Stanford. Then I went to the University of Iowa, where I ended up taking a Ph.D. Travel? Well, back and forth and up and down around this country and in Europe briefly after I got out of school.

Have you ever been in the Armed Services?

No, I was 4-F, luckily . . . I had osteomyelitis, Mickey Mantle's disease.

What influence do you feel European writers . . . either in translation or in the original language . . . have had on American poetry?

I don't know. To find something new and strange—and you can find it in the poetry of other languages—ought to be stimulating. I don't know what effect or influence reading poetry in other languages has had on me. I have found some interesting images—one of these I sort of borrowed from a Chinese poem, that nobody knows—but that is about as far as I can say for sure. I know that a French poet named Guillevic has had some influence on me. There is a feeling that you can now do something other than what you could have done if you hadn't read these other poets. Certainly you don't want to imitate. I don't want to imitate poets who write in other languages any more than I would want to imitate poets who write in my language; but I can perhaps learn something intangible from them. I don't think I can be more specific.

Would you compare the creativity involved in translating the work of others and attempting to transfer beauty from one language to another with that of writing poetry in your own language?

The essential element of translation, as far as I can see, is that one has to have a sort of generally creative sensibility to begin with, rather than the ability to invent anew. One oughtn't to want to be specifically "creative" when translating. If one concentrates on invention, I think one is tempted to let one's own personality betray the original text, which means that it is no longer what I would call translation.It may be something interesting, but it isn't a translation. I stress the importance, however, of an *essentially* creative sensibility. A scholar may know the language better, but one who is in the habit of writing poetry is more likely to come up with a readable and true translation, provided he has a certain respect and feel for the original text. I prefer reading translations by the poets. One of the best translators of his time is Wilbur.

How did you learn to write poetry?

I don't know. I didn't learn from teachers, unless you could call your friends your teachers. And the books you read. Winters taught me something about meters. It has to be self-teaching, I think, mainly, but then I believe any teaching has to be self-teaching. I don't think that the teaching of poetry is so much different from the teaching of humanities or any of the arts. What could be taught quickly and easily is what can be mastered by rote, and anything that pertains to what Western writers call the spirit can't be taught by rote. The first semester of a foreign language can be taught fairly easily; first semester arithmetic, too. But painting? Yes, how to mix colors, but . . .

How do you write? Do you set a few hours aside every day and discipline yourself . . . more or less call these your writing hours, or do you write while "inspired"?

Having observed part of an Iowa City day, you can see that anyone here might have a hard time maintaining a daily discipline. There was a period of about two-and-one-half months when I was able to spend three or four hours every morning writing . . . that was in the spring of 1958. Now I look forward to summers and the years off. Sometimes I "write" on the fly while driving between home and office. I wish it could be different, but that's the way it goes.

One of the groups of poets that have received a lot of attention these past years is the Beat poets. What, in your opinion, caused this school of poetry to come into being? What is its origin?

I don't know. I didn't know any of them. I can't imagine what was going on in their heads, and what was going on in their lives. I only know by gossip and reading about it in Luce publications. Some of it remains modestly interesting eight or nine years after the time. If you can make the question more specific, maybe I can give a little more specific answer. Like what do I think of "Howl"? The one assignment I have given in a poetry writing class was to write a sonnet, for which the first prize was a copy of "Howl," which seemed to me to be the two extremes then going. I thought by rubbing up together they might produce something a little more interesting than either of the two extremes. A friend of mine, Bob Mezey, once read a section of "Howl" on a tape recorder to the background of one of the Brandenburg concertos. It sounded lovely. But I feel something is lacking in much of the poetry of the so-called Beats or the so-called poetry of the Beats, whichever.

What qualities are lacking?

That sort of quality which might have been supplied, for instance, by the Brandenburg concerto. There aren't any poems from that movement, if it was a movement, that I love, as you can gather, but there are a few which interest me, mildly. Very mildly.

What do you feel should be the stance of the poet in political matters?

No special stance that I can see. As a citizen the poet should stand where he thinks he ought to stand. And I personally think he ought to stand on the left, with skepticism, some scorn and some contempt for whatever is abominable in our present institutions of government. But this really doesn't have anything to do with being a poet. If he is a poet and feels this way, as a citizen, he may write poems which express some of his feelings about the government. It would probably be fine to be able to bring your profession and art in line with your activities and action in all spheres, but that is hard for many people, including me.

What poets do you think influenced you?

Practically all the poets in all the anthologies in all the languages. . . .

Do you have a book that's coming out?

Next February.*

Mr. Bell was saying earlier that he thought there's been a change in your style. Would you care to comment?

There is in America, I think, a sort of loosening up in poetry. In techniques, for instance . . . also subject matter. This is generally true, and I think it may be true also of my own work. I don't know whether to attribute it to an easy swinging along with fashions, or to a change in my life, or to the fact that I've read other poets, or to a willed desire to do things differently. All of these factors perhaps entered into it. But how can you, unless you've undergone something like a religious conversion, as a few poets in my generation seem to have done, attribute it to one factor only? The process is more gradual—nothing, for me, like being struck by light on the way to Damascus. It's much harder to say how things happen, or if they did happen even. In my first book there are no poems in free verse, but I had all along been trying to write in free verse, though I had never finished anything. Now I have finished a few. To decide to loosen up and write differently may not be so much a deliberate choice at a certain point in one's career; it may be a public matter. It may have something to do with the way the world is going, or it may just be literary. All I know for sure is that there are some poets now, including me, who have found that it is becoming somewhat easier to do something in a loose form. I don't see any occasion for moral fervor in this, as some do. This all may have something

---

*Night Light.

7

to do with the process of maturing—statistically, that is—or finding more confidence in handling any type of verse at all. I really don't know. Certainly you don't want to keep doing the same things over and over, things you have already done.

You were talking about unfinished poems . . . What keeps a poem unfinished? Do you lose interest or do you find that you can't go where you wanted to? What exactly halts a poem short of completion for you?

Very hard to say. Most of my unfinished poems . . . it isn't that I've lost interest in them. I'm about as narcissistic and egoistic regarding my own work as any poet. Once I've got something started, I tend to like it and want to carry on with it. But sometimes you can't make up enough good lines. I rarely know beforehand where a poem is going to end. I don't know what the whole idea of it is going to be before I get started. It's not as if I knew by reaching the city limits and the signs saying that this is such and such a town, that I'd arrived at my destination. I've published a few things I've thought of as fragments.

We were talking to some of the students in the workshop last night. They told us you had recently written some plays. Is this true, and would you care to comment about them if it is?

Well, the plays they saw would be the ones shown here last week. Last year I was lucky enough to have a grant which allowed me to work with a theater company out in San Francisco with the idea that I would write some plays. I wrote one play in verse, because I didn't believe it was possible, and I guess I more or less proved to other people that it wasn't possible . . . although I proved to myself that it was. I like it, in other words; nobody else did.* A longer one, given here last week, was in prose, which seems easier to write for the stage, and prose is what I probably will use for anything

---

*A little later this was to become the libretto for Edward Miller's opera, *The Young God*.

intended for the stage. I think plays can be wonderful. You have in plays a much clearer sense of an immediately apprehensible form than you do in, say, a short story or a novel. In this way it resembles poetic form somewhat, and that's one of the aspects which fascinate me. I can feel the form of a play, the rhythm within a play, more easily than I can in a short story. I've tried writing short stories, too. I can't imagine how anybody ever writes a novel . . . without becoming lost in the form itself long before the novel's done.

Would you describe in more detail some of the plays you have done?

Well, one of the plays given here last week, "A Dream of Don Juan," was meant to be funny.

Do you think it was?

It was somewhat funny. It wasn't nearly as funny to other people as it was to me. I saw jokes in every line and not everyone else did. Not anybody.

Isn't humor difficult to write? Especially when you consider that every individual has his own personal ideas about what constitutes humor?

Humor, simple humor, must be awfully easy to write. I know that in every rehearsal where an audience was present, and at both of the performances, the line which got the biggest laugh was the line I made up last in the play, simply because the character needed more time to climb around on stage, and what easier way than to put in a simple gag? And I think I could have made a structure of simple gags with relative ease. But I was interested in something a little beyond humor.

I think of a poem as a final process that the poet has finished and has given to the public in its final form . . . they can do little to change it. However, the play doesn't seem that way because you write more than just language and dialogue . . . you are writing expressions, acting instructions, etc., that someone else may misinterpret.

Well, that's part of the fun of it. In a play you use sound that is non-verbal sound. You put in lights, costumes, movements, and stage directions. You can plan all this as the playwright, and of course the director is never going to execute all of your wishes, but at least he can come close. You're playing with a whole set of elements . . . you can play with them formally too. . . . Consider the end of the Don Juan play we were talking about, for instance. An image has been built up, indirectly, I hope, that riding horseback is the same as making love . . . now this is never stated, directly, but at the end of the play a statue climbs down from his pedestal and invites the woman, who's been weeping, to join him on the horse, and off they ride downstage to take their final bow. (It is an equestrian statue.) Now there are some visual elements there, and something of an image, and a sound effect . . . a horse whinnies. You can plan the combination of these elements in a simple and comical way. At the first afternoon performance the sound-effects man missed his cue for the whinny, and a part of the whole texture was lost, and as a matter of fact, the audience found this less funny than when that evening we got the sound effect cued in properly. The non-verbal ingredients are part of the *poetry* of the form.

You made a remark that you didn't take this play seriously. Why?

Well, in part I wrote it as an exercise to see what you could do in combining all sorts of theatrical elements. I wrote the music too, which I really enjoyed doing. I helped plan part of the scenery and stage setting. The set involved mirrors which were supposed to reflect light back into the eyes of the audience, so they would have trouble looking at it. George Starbuck made a lovely mobile out of small mirrors which kept turning and revolving and flashing in the eyes of the audience. These things didn't work out perfectly, but you get some idea of the combination of elements that you can, really, try to compose.

Many poets are currently involved in the Vietnam situation through read-ins on various campuses. What do you feel should be the stance of the poet or yourself on political matters?

If a poet feels strongly enough about the situation, and has written some poems which reflect that feeling, then I think he ought to take part. On the other hand, he shouldn't feel that he has a special privilege as a poet to declare truths of a political nature. If I hadn't written any political poems—I've written only a few—then I would feel like I ought to be carrying a banner, or writing letters or something like that. I do believe in doing what can be done. I don't think much can be done, as a matter of fact, and I'm sorry about this. I wish I knew of a better way than carrying banners, writing letters, and reading poems.

What poets in America do you feel are either overrated or underrated in relation to their respective talents?

I think I'd rather talk about those I think are underrated, if I can think of any. Most poets do have their admirers now . . . poets older than I am. . . . I think Elder Olson is underrated. A few years back I edited the works of Weldon Kees, who was certainly underrated at that time, and I think still is. Among my contemporaries, Henri Coulette has to have been underrated since, until this year, he hadn't published a book. Phil Levine I like, too. Poets younger than I am: Mark Strand and several around here. Too many perhaps to specify without offending.

Do you think there are any "major poets" writing today?

Anyone who's been called a major poet recently would have to be overrated.

You don't feel there are any major poets writing in America?

No, I can't say that I do.

Do you feel any show possibilities of becoming major poets?

I hope they all do. Dozens of people in America have written brilliant and beautiful poems, and that's about all one can say. Of people who are still writing much, one of the best is John Berryman, who keeps getting better. I don't think this "getting better" can be said about anybody else I think of offhand. For instance, Karl Shapiro, whom I used to regard very highly, seems to me to be getting worse and worse. Even that, though, may be a sign of health; if he'd continued to write poems like those in his first few books, by this time it would be very tiring. Berryman is fascinating, I think. I feel it is really possible to learn from his poetry, to learn a good many things.

I don't know if this is true, but I've heard that when Berryman reads his dream songs he treats them very humorously, laughs a lot and gives the impression of not taking them seriously at all. Do you think or know if this is true?

I've never heard him read. But he does put funny things in them, of course, like "Woof," that are personal and characteristic of him. And to have put the poems in this sort of dramatic guise, to have mixed up methods is his way of pushing the material off, getting a distance. Well, sure, there's a lot of sadness . . . it's a mixed mode of expression . . . which is one of the ways of being modern . . . it's a tragicomical, historical, political . . . I can't remember how Polonius describes the playing of the players . . . the most complicated description he used would probably describe the dream songs. They have something for everybody, something of every kind.

Do you feel that grants, aids, or other kinds of prizes can ever affect a person's poetry?

Well, if you were told in advance that you would win a certain award for writing poems of a certain kind and you went ahead and wrote those poems, and won that award, that would be silly and awful. But as it actually happens you have written the poems first and if you win a prize, it can't change the poems. Now it may change the person, but this is unpredictable. Most awards don't carry so much prestige that it should alter anybody's character seriously to have won or lost. Grants are good in that they clear time for your writing, if you weren't born rich.

Since you don't feel there are any major American poets writing today, whom would you classify, in the past, as a major American poet? Would you include Frost and Stevens?

Yes, sure, I would include those two certainly . . . Eliot, if he's American, Pound as a young man. Williams . . . I may be leaving out somebody.

Has there been a major woman poet in America?

Emily Dickinson without a doubt. The most interesting woman writing poetry today is Elizabeth Bishop.

Do you have any personal opinions as to why there are so few women poets?

It's probably something to do with American society. It probably has something to do with very large indefinable things . . . it certainly can't have anything to do with supposing that men are better than women, are smarter than women . . . it's the result of history, of culture.

Do you feel that there is talent being wasted, or don't you feel there is any talent there to waste?

The talent must be wasted . . . maybe there will be, the next generation, more women poets than men. Women live longer and their place in society is getting to be freer and more open.

Yet there was Emily Dickinson, a major poet, and a woman writing a long time ago before woman's place was free and open.

She didn't have children, didn't have to go out and get a job. Her household responsibilities were very small . . . she had only to please her father or keep quiet around him, a little baking . . . and it is possible to do that and then go off to your room and write a poem, *if* you happen to be a genius. I'm surprised that more American spinsters haven't written poetry. Perhaps their sisters only failed to look in the bureau. Vinnie Dickinson looked.

(1966)

An Interview with Geoffrey Clark, Robert Crotty, and Robert L. McRoberts

As a first question: formerly, you wrote fiction?

That was a long time ago. I was trying to write poems, but I wasn't succeeding. So I wrote a couple of stories. Though what I suppose you might call promising for a young writer, they don't really stand up.

Did you choose poetry then?

Yes, I had always wanted to write poems. Apparently during one brief period of my life I was able to write fiction better. And then, when I found out more or less how to write poems, I wrote poems.

Do you have any strong feelings about the possibilities and limitations of each? Do you feel, for instance, that you can better express yourself in the poem? Or do you feel that the poem is made for a certain type of expression you're interested in?

It's not that so much. It's a matter of doing what I could do. And since my preference really lay with poems, when I could write poems, then I did write them. Obviously fiction seems much more capable of dealing with people in time and in relation with one another and with events that grow out of one another—sequential things. And that's one of the greatest pleasures in reading fiction, to get a sense of life unfolding. Poems very rarely give such a sense. Partly it's because poems nowadays are shorter, I suppose, but even when poems were longer you got very few poems which give . . .

Even the narrative poems?

I think so. What poems do anything like what you get in, say, *Anna Karenina* or *Middlemarch?* In the nineteenth century there's "Michael"; perhaps "Dora" by Tennyson, which no one seems to know. You didn't really have novels at the time of the truly long poem like *The Faerie Queen* or *Paradise Lost.* All sorts of big questions are involved. What happened in society that made the novel possible? But the poems people write now just bite off a little bit of something to chew, and they tend to be small poems. And I think it's much easier to apprehend the form of a poem from either the point of view of the reader or of the writer than something as big as a novel. One types a novel for many months, and though it may take me months to finish a poem, I'm not doing the kind of physical labor that will produce bulk in the long run. What you become concerned with in the poem is different. Now one of the things you might try to do in a poem is to give a sort of quick glimpse into the kind of life you might get in a novel. But it would depend on a quick penetration and getaway, rather than on spreading everything out, putting things in. Leaving things out would be more the way of the poem, I think. A novel accumulates. It seems to me that's one of the pleasures of the novel; it keeps accumulating detail and fact and action, and a poem tends, these days anyway, to exclude. There have been exceptions, but I think it is a general tendency to leave things out instead of to put things in.

Does the prose poem "Orpheus Opens His Morning Mail" show any relationship between your prose and poetry?

No. As I say, my fiction was such a long time ago it would be odd to expect much connection. For one thing, I myself have changed. At the time of the prose poems, I was interested in breaking up the kind of poem I had been bound to. One of the ways of doing that was to take a kind of subject or attitude that might have been put into what I thought of as verse, and to put it into prose instead. There's another thing about the prose poems in *Night Light*. I had been trying, as a lot of people have tried, to write in a simpler and plainer style in verse. I thought, since I believe things tend to operate by contraries, that I could allow myself to be more elegant or ornate in prose than in poetry. I wrote some fairly ornate sentences in those prose poems that I don't think I would have allowed myself in verse at the time.

Do you feel that in Night Light, *with the free verse and syllabics, you've gotten away from the forms of* The Summer Anniversaries?

I always wanted to do everything, everything there was to do. Others must want that too. Once you've written a sonnet, unless you plan to write a whole sequence of sonnets, why write another? Once you've written a sestina, why write another, unless you can find something new in the form to work out?

If you came across something now that would lend itself to a sonnet or a sestina, would you be interested in using that?

A sestina, maybe, not a sonnet. I don't know exactly why that is, but I think it's a prejudice.* Many people have prejudices like that. Brainwashing, maybe.

Do you feel that moving from traditional forms to free verse is a normal progression, a way of training yourself?

Well, it seems clear enough from recent literary history that you don't really have to prepare by going through routine and traditional forms. But there is another way of looking at all this, too. The modern convention is to write free verse. By

---

*Which I have only recently conquered.—1983.

now it is *the* convention, the one poets start with. So it might work the other way around—start with free verse, graduate to the meters. But to the young poet meters seem so hard!

Do you have a sense of form with syllabics?

Syllabics are a guide, a clue, an aid to the writer in establishing for himself a sense of form to work with. But I don't think they are of much use to the reader. Not the way most syllabics are written, certainly. They don't seem to do anything for the ear of the *reader*. Perhaps they have had something to do with shaping the idea—for the *writer*. I look on syllabics as a writer's form. That may be true of all conventions in verse, but it seems to me more obviously true of syllabics than of anything else I've come across. On the other hand, blank verse seems to be something you can hear as a *reader*, really and truly hear. Sometimes all too clearly, of course, too thuddily.

What's the process of a Justice poem now?

It depends. There's one group I've been working on, a group of portraits, in which I start—formally—with the idea of a line based on a six-syllable count. (They're what I mentioned earlier, attempts to give a quick glimpse into the kind of life a novel might deal with—short novels, you might say, very short.) However, as for the syllable count, I've varied that from the base of six—as few as three, as many as eight. If the line goes longer than eight it doesn't seem to look right as a line with the others. So I make adjustments. The result is a sort of *loose syllabics*. One might call it that. I've noticed other poems that seem to be written in a kind of loose syllabics. Frost said something about "loose iambics" once as one of the kinds of verse you could write. Well, syllabics are loose enough to start with, except for the sheer, strict count of them. But I think this is a possibility—loose syllabics. Why not? It's one possible way of thinking of the verse line and in fact it's a plausible enough way of describing one of the mainstreams of free verse, one in which the accents aren't intended to sound loud and chantlike, and the lines tend to be of similar lengths.

How do you feel about the reading of your poems? Do you feel that they're best apprehended when read aloud? Do you write them to be read aloud rather than to be read silently?

No, I write them to be read on the page. Others, I guess, write poems to be read aloud. But I should qualify this bald assertion. As I write a poem for the page I would like for its potential of sound to be available for the person reading silently. Eventually, if it comes to be said aloud, it should sound okay—it should sound like somebody speaking, and speaking well. Most of the time. Once in a while like singing. Never like declaiming or shouting. Or preaching. Never.

Has reading aloud affected your poems, in the way that it has Robert Lowell, for example?

No, it hasn't. I don't usually make many mistakes when reading aloud. And when I do, I hear the mistake right away, and I never like it. Now apparently Lowell did like some of his mistakes because it gave him a sense of loosening up the very hard, thuddy iambic pentameter line he had been writing in. It hasn't happened to me that way.

I was interested in "Early Poems." Do you really feel now that rhymes and meters tend to paralyze?

Oh, the meters *can* paralyze, but they don't have to. I'm playing around with a very conventional attitude in that poem, not necessarily my attitude.

The other day you were saying that it takes you such a long time between books. . . . Is it something in the process of your poems?

It may have more to do with sloth. And I wasn't born rich, so I have to earn a living. Nor am I a fast writer, though I wish I were and have tried conscientiously to become faster. Some people I know don't feel right unless they can finish at least the first draft of a poem when they sit down the first time. I've tried very hard to do that and have succeeded a few times, but only a few. Then there are some who just don't believe in revising very much. I happen to be a constant reviser, and that takes a long time. For me the process of writing a poem is ordinarily a long one. I have finished perhaps three poems in my life quickly. That is, after adolescence, when everything comes—and goes—quickly.

Your poems have a restraint and control that seem to suggest a conscious, deliberate artist working on them. Is there any time when you want to free yourself from this restraint or control?

I don't think I feel the need to let go. Nowadays people may think of that as a flaw. I don't.

"To the Hawks" is an antiwar poem. How do you feel about protest poems?

I felt very sick at the time I was writing it, and it was a sort of discharge—to get something out of my system. If I were ever tempted to write about violence, this poem might stand as symptomatic of what my tactics would be. Even though I felt very strongly about the war, I didn't want to approach the subject directly. So I tried to write as quiet a poem as I could—about violence.

In "Men at Forty" is the word mortgaged *in the last line a deliberate intrusion of prosaic reality?*

It is meant to sound a little out of context.

It seems to jar the reader out of the mood of the poem.

Maybe that's a good idea. If it does, then the end is surely one of the right places, esthetically, to be jarred. But it's not at all as if the word were a sudden obscenity or great shock. You find a sort of technical language frequently in Shakespeare's sonnets, Donne, the word *coal* at the end of a Herbert poem, etc.

Previous to that in the poem you have this beautiful imagery, like "beneath him now like the deck of a ship." But then you get to the last line, "Behind their mortgaged houses," and it seems to break a whole sort of aura of mysteriousness. It is almost as if there are rites being performed, and then we come upon this very hard, concrete word.

I'd like you to feel tempted in reading this poem to convert this over into a rite or mystery also—this last line. One of the things that happen to people is that they get tied up in something like a house. Really, the people, the men at forty, are, as the image works out, inside houses all along. And the houses become, I'd like to think, almost an image for their bodies, the men themselves, extensions. It is the hardest fact given in the poem, and that's why it's saved for the end. As an example of what I mean, there is a road in Iowa City,* a place up on a hill, with nice houses, many of them heavily mortgaged, I expect. And behind the houses there's this very nice slope down into the woods from which you hear the sounds of the woods. The men who own these houses, a good many of them, happen to be around forty, and though I wasn't thinking of them in particular, it seems symbolic to me that they should be perched up there. It's a high point and yet . . . I wanted the geography and the physical facts of lives like these to be convertible into images having meaning, the things themselves to be symbolic.

In your poetry now, do you feel that you're still exploring forms? Do you still like to create forms and write out of those?

---

*The very street—Ridge Road—on which I was to build my first house eight years later! Mortgaged, of course.—1983.

21

Yes. Partly because there's something of the game in all this, and games give pleasure. The game has no end beyond itself—virtually the definition of the esthetic. And games can give you a pleasure remotely like what you're after when you're at play with a form, or at work on it—whatever.

(1969)

An Interview with Gregory Fitz Gerald and William Heyen

Why did you use Katmandu as the locale for "Here in Katmandu"?

Katmandu was the starting point of the expedition which originally conquered Mt. Everest. I got my information out of the movie that was made about the expedition—Louis Mac-Neice wrote the commentary—a film which impressed me with its visual magnificence. It seemed to be providing images for a poem, and so I tried to use them in a way that touched a subject which had caught me.

Were you interested in human aspiration?

Yes, that's a way of putting it. Being born in flat country—Florida—and reading books about climbing: all that probably had more to do with the poem than any largish abstraction would. You might say that geography provides metaphors for the human. But if any of my poems moralize, as I suppose some of them unavoidably do, "Here in Katmandu" moralizes on the theme of failure and success. You wanted to conquer Everest, you did it, and then, either you felt an emptiness, or you didn't like what you came back to. But you didn't much like what you had found in the process either.

And then there's the sense of letdown in descending from any heights, or from any emotional experience of that magnitude?

That's the underlying theme which the word *down* keeps emphasizing.

Would you say that the voice of this poem is typical of your work?

Yes and no. I hope that most of my poems have something of what I could recognize as my own voice, whether other people could or not. It's a voice that is pitched somewhat impersonally, which is usually the way I speak in poems.

Are there any changes other than stylistic between your early work and your later poems?

I don't recognize any really profound changes, though there may be some. The formal apparatus of the poems, which I'm immensely concerned with, is different. Since form and content operate together, what's being said is necessarily going to sound and actually be a little different, too. When I began to learn something about writing, I was interested in the forms that others had shown could be used, and could be used interestingly. My interest in very ingenious and elaborate forms is connected to this desire that seems to be natural with me: to displace the self from the poem—not to remove it entirely, but to displace it, in some degree. A fairly elaborate apparatus of form does just that.

Do you spend a considerable amount of time revising your work?

A good deal of time, yes, usually because I'm not always lucky the first time through a poem, and I want to make it better. If a passage or a line or a phrase doesn't sound good, even though it seemed at one point an important part of the argument or presentation of a scene, then I'd be inclined to leave it out. It's a poem, after all, and it wants to sound good.

Are you worried about the personal element in poetry?

Not as far as my own poems are concerned. I think that whatever character or temperament I have enters the better poems unavoidably and so I don't find myself taking a lot of trouble trying to get myself in. I go to far more trouble trying to leave myself out.

Certainly your poetry isn't as personal as, say, Heart's Needle *by W. D. Snodgrass.*

Heart's Needle is a fine book, with many fine poems in it. You probably know the essay Snodgrass wrote after the book came out. It contains a passage, which I might try paraphrasing, to the effect that we who were brought up in that generation were raised on a criticism which showed us how really to examine a poem and understand it, or even how to put it together, but that time has passed now; the final test is sincerity. Now that is simply not the kind of poetry I write.

You spoke earlier about creating new forms of your own. Could you describe something of what you've been doing recently in this line?

I don't, myself, want to use the term "organic form"—that's been batted about too much, it seems to me—and anyhow that isn't the way I look at it. But the forms do make themselves up as the poems get written. Is that too nebulous a description?

There's a sense in which our study of literature has become an attempt to try to enunciate for ourselves the relationship between the thing that is said and the way it is said, and how these two finally merge. It's almost impossible to talk about it; it's something you feel, I suppose.

It is very hard to express. If a poem comes out as good, then there was no other way it could have been said. We have that kind of faith.

You've written a poem called "The Assassination." This is a poem about the death of John Kennedy, isn't it?

No, it's about the assassination of Robert Kennedy. Things apparently have to happen two or three times before I begin to catch on. By the time John Kennedy's brother was assassinated, I felt something of what assassination was like, what it could mean. Also for the first time I had a television set, so I could see the events in an immediate and scary way. So I thought—I feel something about this; I have something to say about it; maybe this is one of those public events one can write about. It wasn't quite that mechanical, but I did feel I could write a poem about it. Because I usually approach things indirectly, I didn't want merely to say, "Well, this is terrible!" I was also interested in the notion of playing around with chance, partly because of an acquaintance with John Cage, I guess. So about this time I started writing words down on three-by-five note cards, which happened to be lying around the house. And writing down sentence models—syntax blanks or abstracts—on another set of cards. Once the cards had been shuffled, I found several sentences that I could then complete with a word from the other stack. I managed in this way to approach a subject which I would have found hard to approach directly. To aim chance in the right direction I filled cards with words I heard on TV news broadcasts. I'm sorry if that description is not too clear, but the process was both complicated and improvised. I dated the poem June 5, 1968, in part to insist on its topicality.

The central image hidden in "The Assassination" is blood, is it not?

Yes, it is blood. It *runs* all through the poem, until perhaps the last few very short sentences.

Have you written many poems using the chance method you describe?

About three and a half.

Do you plan to write more?

I've tried shuffling the cards, but I haven't had any luck.

But what does it enable you to do?

To put it simply, it frees the imagination. I don't tell myself I have to accept what chance determines. There may be poets who would accept whatever comes up in the cards. I reserve the right of final approval of what chance tells me to say.

(1970)

An Interview with Wayne Dodd
and Stanley Plumly

I would like to hear you talk about what you think is the change between where you were with the first book, Summer Anniversaries, *and where you've come to with the latest,* Departures. *The poems are formally different, of course, but what about the change in the presence of Don Justice in the poems?*

The very nature of the question makes it hard for me to judge that. I can speak of intentions. I haven't ever intended to put myself directly into the poems, not in any of the poems I've written. I've always felt it was an author's privilege to leave himself out if he chose—and I so chose, contrary to the choice of certain friends and contemporaries. I suppose I must have been acting originally under the powerful influence of early essays by Eliot in that, and, insofar as it was a conscious choice, seeking the—I've forgotten the phrase—"the efface-ment of the personality."* The self. I have in my poems con-scientiously effaced my self, I think, if not my personality. But I might be the last to know if I could be recognized as a person in the poems or not. I am often speaking in some imagined or borrowed voice. I may be writing about things I know personally, even intimately, but to a certain degree I want to pretend that it is otherwise.

---

*"A continual extinction of personality . . . not the expression of personality, but an escape from personality."

I understand that, but I was thinking about the obvious topographical difference—the simple fact that so many more of them speak in the assumed first person, whatever the character, and even—well, let's say in the poem "Variations on a Text by Vallejo."

Yes, that's true, I do assume it there . . .

Which I find a tremendously moving, powerful poem.

But the Vallejo itself is powerful and moving, and I was moved to try to appropriate some of its power, I suppose. Because that is a case, I think, of a borrowed voice. And borrowing the voice allows me, it seems, to speak of myself more directly, more objectively, because the voice is not mine. Not simply mine. Probably more than other poets I know, I play games in my poems (as I do in life), and one of the unwritten rules of the game for me, as I like it played, is that you can risk this much personality or that much confession if the voice is promised to be that of someone else to start with. Even without my recognizing it at the time of writing, that may be one of the reasons I am sometimes literary in choice of subjects, in taking off from other people's texts. Something in the works of others, I suppose, gets to me personally, affords me another perspective, the objectivity and distance I like, so that it is as if I could say to myself, let me use his experience as an image of my own, and I won't have to use mine. But using his turns out to be another experience for me, so it really *will* be mine in the end. I'm not making that very clear, I guess, but it must be part of a psychological mechanism. I think it works that way. A defense mechanism.

Okay. Does that borrowing occur in "Absences" and "Presences" too?

"Absences," as far as I know, is not a borrowed voice, not beyond the first phrase, at least. "Presences," as one may easily recognize, is a borrowing from Vallejo again, but a less open borrowing and therefore not acknowledged.

Well, granting and assuming that there is a borrowed voice in some of these more personal-seeming poems, I wonder what you think of the different kind of poetry that you're generating and creating by the simple use of that, as distinct from a more objective kind, a more distant poetry that you were writing fifteen years ago.

Some of the poems in my second book, *Night Light*, are probably more objective transcriptions of what would appear to be reality than anything I can remember, offhand, in the first book, or than most of the things in the latest book, *Departures*. I don't know quite how that came about, but I have wanted, as many poets must have, to try all kinds of things in writing, and I wouldn't be satisfied with, say, finding a formula for writing a poem and then doing it a second time, except perhaps in a short series of related poems, with the end already in sight; or, if I were, I'd rather not know that I was doing it. I would like to write different kinds of things all the time. I do think *Departures* is different from *Summer Anniversaries* or from *Night Light,* and both the second and third books are, I like to think, developments, even improvements upon, *departures* from, the first book, which was largely, I believe, apprentice work. It proved to me, if not to anyone else, that I could go through the motions of writing poems. I take the motions seriously enough, but more as a demonstration of . . .

Some of those formal sestinas in there, I think, testify in part . . .

Yeah, well, I love sestinas, though not my own particularly. I have no objection to the sestina as an imposed form, and if I could write a sestina easily tonight when I go home, I'd do so, but having done it already I'd have to think the new one would be different somehow. I don't know. Which may be why I won't do it, not tonight, anyhow. Two of the four I attempted in that first book—those are the only ones I have done—resemble each other on the surface: "A Dream Sestina" and "Sestina on Six Words by Kees." They came about in different ways, and so I can think of them as different. But the other two are really *variations* on a sestina base, as it were.

"Here in Katmandu" starts off being a perfect one, but then it changes . . .

What I called it at the time was a free-verse sestina, because the lines varied considerably in length. I wanted to make a pun on "Katmandu" out of the end-word *do*.

I believe you changed the pattern, even, somewhere along the line.

Maybe. I know I did in "A Dream Sestina," because the first ten lines or so of that were dreamed in a real dream and in the second stanza I simply got the order of the end-words wrong, a natural enough mistake for anybody asleep to make, so I had to work it out from there when I woke up. I didn't want to change the "mistake."

But do I understand you right in thinking that part of what you said is that this is not necessarily a one-way street: in other words you come from, say, your apprentice work to the present, but not in a necessarily evolutionary way—developmental, yes, but not necessarily evolutionary?

That's my own sense of it. There are single poems, perhaps even groups of poems, or poems in a certain style, that I would be willing to put aside, but I wouldn't want to be too harsh on any phase of what I've done just because it was one thing instead of the other. You might say I like it all because it's mine. Doesn't everybody feel that way? No, I don't look on it as progress, which would be the term to describe an evolution. If anything, it's more a simple process of continual change and not a progress toward any foreseeable goal of perfection. Partly it must be in response to the pressures in what you might call the culture of the time, you know. I think most people are sensitive to fashions, literary fashions, and I believe I have been too. I don't feel guilty about it.

But isn't part of that change from the first book to the second and the third due to your reading of certain Spanish poets?

They certainly were an influence on some of the poems in the third book, yes.

I was thinking of "The Man Closing Up," for example.

That's from the French, of course, a sort of leap I take from Guillevic's poem. No, I couldn't have written that poem without having read some Guillevic, even though my poem happened to be written without my having a copy of his poems around. I remembered his poem. I had translated it very roughly one afternoon, about, oh, ten months before I sat down to write my own version, and of course without planning at the time to write a poem from it, and I remembered something about it. I certainly remembered the *strong* sense of a definite style that Guillevic had given me. And I was interested in seeing if I could do something similar in style in my own language, in English.

That was really my question: What is it that you found in the translation of, let's say, French?

I thought I found in some poets various possibilities for style which I had not found in American and English poets or in myself. But I hope the styles I saw corresponded somehow to things in myself, and potentially in the language. Not altogether foreign. I'm not *sure* that that's so.

This may be dumb, but what do you mean by style? If we were talking about prose, I'd think I'd have a better sense . . .

Well, there were certain features of style in Guillevic, for instance, in the poems of his that I liked, which I had not seen handled in the same way by American or English poets. He did write in the skinny line, the short line, which a lot of American poets have done, but he did not sound at all like William Carlos Williams, which most skinny-line poems in English tend to do. He used particulars, for example, but did not make a big point of it. They might appear or they might not. He used plain language and, I suppose, even some some-what slangy turns of phrase, which might make him resemble Williams, but the total effect of the way he put all these to-gether was so unlike Williams that it was refreshing, not that I don't admire Williams himself greatly. I suppose, now that I think of it, I was interested in the fact that his poems looked as if they should sound like Williams and they didn't. There was a sort of challenge to me to find out what the secret of that was, and I tried to invent or duplicate that kind of effect for myself. For, as far as I know, the first time in English. The last time, too, I guess.

But in those poems in the second book, and I think this is true of many things in Departures, *there's a lot more breathing room, a lot more—the current cliché is "open-endedness." Let's say there's a very clear sense of silence surrounding the poems. And inside the poems, too.*

I used to try to put in all the logical steps, and all the connec-tions, and to try to finish the statement with a conclusion. I was thinking, before coming over here tonight, that I used to be more certain about things in my youth than I am now. Whatever changes may have taken place may be related to that—some principle of uncertainty. Most poems written in 1970, say, were more like that—more "open-ended"—than most poems written in 1950, and it may simply be that I was going along with the tide of the time. But I am generally more wary of "statement" now, of announcing any conclusions, in verse or prose, than I was when starting out—in 1952.

Despite your still-professed interest in the sestina (which I believe I have, too), nonetheless, you don't write many sestinas.

No, I haven't written any for, oh, nearly twenty years.

And your commitment to that kind of formal pattern certainly seems less than it once was.

As to commitment, yes. I have been interested not in what passes for organic form, which I have never understood as applied to literature, but in finding what I would prefer to acknowledge as literary forms, perhaps ones that have not been much used before, however. One of the reasons for my interest in poems in other languages was a result, I believe, of the illusion of perceiving in them literary forms which I had not encountered in English. Now, I don't mean something that you could call, say, a sonnet. Take an example. I like to talk specifically, when I can. There's a section of an Alberti poem about his early school days called "Collegio, S. J." I first encountered it in translation in *Modern European Poetry*, and then I read it in Spanish, and I noticed that the translator had altered what seemed to me a crucial part of the syntactical form of the poem, an alteration which, to my mind, very drastically changed the rhetorical force of the original structure. There had been an address to the sea in the poem, at the beginning of the last paragraph: "O Sea," he says, or, rather, just "Sea." In the Spanish there is no "O." And the translator had put this at the *beginning* of the poem, and just such a simple shift as that seemed to me to eliminate a great virtue in the original text, in which, for line after line, maybe fifteen lines—I don't remember the exact figures—Alberti had been addressing something or someone, you didn't know who or what. It was very mysterious and engaging, and suddenly he says, "Sea, you used to come up to our classroom." And I thought that was a magical moment, which the translator had obliterated. In the interest of clarity, perhaps. Well, I was interested in seeing if that postponement of the apostrophe, as at the least a small syntactical or rhetorical form, truly had the inherent power I suspected, and if what I thought I found there in the Spanish might also be used in English. I think I found that it could be, in a poem called "Cool Dark Ode." That kind of thing—small things often—but that sort of thing is one way in which I think I was borrowing from foreign poets, things that have to do more with rhetoric or structure than content or attitude.

As long as we're talking about form and things, here's one of those impossible questions I wanted to ask you. What determines a line in unmetered verse, do you think?

That does appear to depend on whim, and I think you might say the duty of the poet is to enforce his whim, so that it comes close to being a principle. And one that can be perceived. Otherwise, I find it boring to see the text broken up as lines. Many free-verse poets, obviously, have broken lines according to phrase length, according to phrase division. That would seem to me the most conventional way of doing it. Stevens' free verse divides by phrase. And that's a reasonable method of proceeding. Others do it differently. Williams often did not break by phrase, as we commonly understand it. He had some other rhythm, I suppose, in his mind or ear, and yet I believe that his aberrant line divisions—aberrant in the sense that they do not obey the phrase length, the phrase division—seem in many poems to reach toward the level of principle, to be perceptible as significant. Other poets have broken lines in order to be witty. Williams does this sometimes, consciously or not—to get a double sense out of either the last word or the first phrase in the next line. Marvin Bell used to do that frequently in his earlier poems, and Creeley has done it. Other people have done it. I find it difficult to understand the mystique of line lengths obeying the breath. I just don't understand that, though some people profess to. I should think, in that case, that if the poet lived long enough and developed emphysema, his lines would become shorter, more ragged, more desperate. Fewer.

It suggests that Creeley is terribly asthmatic.

I didn't mean to suggest that. Must free verse be something in which anything goes? I think the things that go are things which you can see as going much in the same way, from line to line, or even, in the body of a poet's work, from poem to poem, so that you can say about the work of X, oh, I see, his lines go like this, and in the work of Y, oh, his lines go like that. If a universal principle for free verse were ever discovered—but that's inconceivable, isn't it?

When you say it's according to a poet's whim, that does somehow suggest, not just arbitrariness, but almost capriciousness.

Surely all of us must have read many poems which seemed absolutely capricious in their manipulation of line length, at least, if nothing else. That might by paradox become principle, perhaps, but I don't think so. Some people don't care, you know, and that's almost their principle. I wouldn't want to mention names. I prefer a poem to be organized.

What does that mean?

First, to have an apprehensible structure. Something that if you were required by law to do so you could describe in other words. Not something merely felt, which I think is likely to be illusion, but something which three reasonable people could all agree had indeed been happening.

I don't understand what would be the difference between saying you establish something as a principle within a poem and saying that you found the physical form for the spiritual event or idea or impulse in the poem. Would they be the same thing?

I suppose they could be, if I could understand the second option, but, you see, I just have a kind of mental block there. I can't understand how the physical could be the form for the spiritual. It may be that I have that kind of difficulty because I don't believe in the spiritual. You know, there is a power in the obvious. That which is hidden I can't see. That may be because I was brought up as a Southern Baptist and lost my faith.

Well, the containing and ordering of energy, would that be the same thing?

That sounds pretty good to me, yes. But again, you might ask the question, "What would the ordering be?"

Where does it come from? That's really the question.

I don't think it comes from some source exterior to the operations of the mind or to the syntactical potential of the language.

Denise Levertov has made the statement somewhere that experience has a pattern, has an order, and that the problem of the poet is to find that.

She must believe that. But whatever pattern my experience has, I can't find it. My experience, my life, may have a certain pattern to it, but if so, it would be so simple to describe that it would be a great bore to describe it, even to bother to mention it. And I'm interested in other matters anyhow. One thing: I'm just not that interested in imposing my sense of self, of my discoveries about the essence of life, on others. I don't like to think of myself as a propagandist or an evangelist.

In other words, understatement is to you, practically, a religious principle.

Yes.

Nevertheless, when one reads the first book and the second book and the third book and sees, maybe not an evolutionary growth, but certainly sees your developmental kind of change, one can still perceive, I think, a kind of unity of voice, or sensibility, which, in fact, is saying something. Maybe not something "spiritual," but nevertheless it has about it certain means, certain content, certain things to say.

I hope so. It seems to me I can see that, sometimes while working on something, but I'm not sure, and I wouldn't want to force it.

But what is being said? By Departures, *it seems to me, you are, obviously, not only deepening whatever it is that makes up your con-*

cern, but, to use Mark Strand's word, it is getting "darker." Is that just a function of age?

Oh, I think it probably is, to tell the truth. One could make moral and philosophical . . . One could say that one has seen deeply into the heart of things, but I'm not sure that's so. Most people, I believe, become sadder as they grow older. And there's plenty of reason to.

Yes. But there is clearly a self being revealed there, even if one is not, in fact, being forced at the reader.

Yes, sure. I probably was too quick to dismiss the self before. If one has enough character, it's going to show in spite of one's attempts to disguise it, as an actor playing a role can be recognized from role to role, even though the name of the character he's playing has changed, or the age of the character, the setting, etc. Something about his own character is going to be visible, or he lacks strength as an actor, and will not get many jobs, and those will be small ones. Given that (and it's the sort of thing one has to have faith in), believing that one's character is there, then it seems to me you can stop worrying about it. And it will show up. If it doesn't, then you throw the poem away. Or others will. So I feel nervous about fingering the self too much, or about others who do. I think it's something that won't disappear.

Would you agree that it has become more visible in your work by the third book, through its own reticence, perhaps?

Well, it's possible that it has. If so, I don't see that it has done so *because* I've been trying to withdraw. That seems contradictory.

Well, I think in a very paradoxical sense the withdrawing is a presence. With the understanding and the reticence the self becomes more and more exposed.

I began to think toward the end of writing those poems, that the effacement of the self could become or had already become a pose, and I wouldn't want to make too much more of it. I threw away some pieces on that theme—a total effacement at last, the pose abandoned. I think some kind of pose is probably being struck in most poems; anybody's. But one of the poses that I prefer to strike is of not striking a pose. It gets pretty elaborate if you start to articulate it. You know what I mean. . . .

One of the things I'd like to talk about out of this kind of conversation is really a difficult, but serious and fundamental matter: namely the source of poetry, the source of the impulse of poetry, maybe in general but particularly in your own poetry. I think you have always had a profound strain of melancholy in your poems, right from the outset. And I wonder, what seems to you to be the source of the poems, the impulse for poetry? Is it loss, that essential presence of time in our perception, the sense that even at the moment of being, we know it's passing?

Something like that, I'm sure. True for me, maybe for others. So far as I can psychologize it, one of the motives for writing is surely to recover and hold what would otherwise be lost totally—memory or experience. Put very simply, so that one might not wholly die. Sometimes I think of poetry as making things. Common enough, surely. And I would like to have made some nice things, beautiful things. And in those beautiful things to have got something I would not like to have forgotten: probably involving my own experience, but perhaps that of others. I'd like to think I could write dramatically about other people, not just the damned self all the time. I like looking at old photographs very much, and I . . . It's not a very high-class analogy—but I would like it if, not directly, but in a similar way, some of the poems I've tried to write were treasurable in the sense that I *know* a photograph can be treasurable. Treasured.

Would you say that your attitude, your feelings, your attitude toward your feeling about what you've written and made would be to say, "these I made" rather than "these I was?"

Oh, I would certainly prefer that.

Let me ask you this: do you think, do you feel that when you're working on one particular poem, you leave out a good deal more than you put in (certainly I feel I'm doing that) but also that in the process you're getting more of that poem in?

Well, what does get in can be more accurately perceived by virtue of the exclusion of those things which did not pertain. I like to try, although I think it's very hard to do—and I don't try to do it so much in life as distinct from art—but I would like to make as much sense out of things as possible. And not to go through art, even if I may be obliged to go through life, confused. I would like to make efforts toward clarity and perceptions truly registered, and . . .

So your poems are an instrument to that end?

Language itself is for me—when I'm being very careful with it, as I am when I'm writing. Not so much when talking. Talking is for social intercourse and pleasure, too, but I think the pleasure is of a different order. For one thing, in art it can last, it can be repeated.

You think that's why you write slowly?

Well, yes, I think that's one of the reasons. I do like to get things right. I don't care nearly so much in conversation. Or in interviews.

I'm just wanting somehow to talk more fundamentally about the distinction between the poet as ongoing poem, which several people live their lives and writing as these days; and the poet as a filter, organiz-

*er, register of experience. I think the American classical poetical dif-
ferentiation is between a Whitman and a Dickinson esthetic.*

I think that makes sense, and obviously, I would belong to
Dickinson's line. . . .

After Departures *what happens?*

I don't know. I really don't know and I'm not as excited about
not knowing as probably I should be. But I—if I write anything more, it will probably be either a reversion to the formal, perhaps even the absolutely formal, or else a number of
dignified prose sentences, one after the other. I really don't
think I'll write many more poems in the mode—or modes—of
Departures or *Night Light* or *Summer Anniversaries.* I wouldn't
find that very thrilling to do, and so I—insofar as I'm looking
for anything—I'm looking for a way to do something a little
different that would still be natural to me. For instance, one
of the reasons the formal possibility interests me a little now is
that I feel that the poems in *Summer Anniversaries,* some of
which were quite formal, were just, for me, demonstrations to
myself that I *could* do something. I now think that I could
handle those things better. And it might be worth doing, for
myself, if not for anyone else. But I'm not sure about that—
just about all I've written since *Departures* has been a long
libretto and a few epigrams, a few fragments. Fragments appeal to me—there's an inevitable pathos about them. Which
may be an unacknowledged reason for the appeal of so much
that's chaotic in art nowdays, unfinished. I might write another libretto, then, or a few more epigrams. Certainly more
fragments—unavoidably.

You think you're getting more interested in the theater, then?

I would be if I could be. I would write a play tomorrow if I
could, but I don't think I could. When one starts out in life—

isn't this true for all of you? It was for me—one thinks the possibilities are infinite. There is nothing you couldn't do. But as time passes, some of the possibilities, obviously, fall away. And you probably can't do them any longer. You might have been able to had you started twenty years before. Really getting immersed, as I got immersed in writing poems, things choose you. I wanted most to write music. I've said that before.

You were a pianist?

I played the piano and a few other instruments, not all that well, but I did study composition for, oh, some while in late adolescence. With Carl Ruggles, incidentally—a fine composer and teacher, though he took very few pupils. He wanted me to study with Hindemith at one time. I must have shown a certain promise but at some essential point I doubted. My sense of rhythm came into question, I think. With me, that is, not with Ruggles. I'd always been writing a little— words, I mean—and I turned to that. But I regret the music.

I'd like to go back with you just a second to something you said a moment ago. I was intrigued by what you said, that after Departures *you didn't know where you would go, maybe to write formal poems, or a series of dignified prose sentences, statements. I wondered why.*

Because that would be something that I haven't done before, and I think it would be a possibility for writing that would be interesting enough to tempt me. I've tried doing it some in private lately. And the first alternative—the strictly formal— because, as I say, I don't think I got it quite right the first time and would like to give myself a second chance.

I was thinking of that second alternative. I understand the first one. Do you find many experiments with the prose poem nowadays interesting?

No. Are they experiments? Really? There was a period when the prose poem did interest me, when not very many people had been doing it. Now the form of the prose poem or the kind of prose poem most people have written in America in the last ten, fifteen years is, as far as I can see, just about used up. The ones that may be interesting right now are of a type that my mind just isn't given to making up—little prose fables. They're different from the standard nineteenth-century French prose poem, which most of the prose poems in America I read and enjoyed really took off from. No, I'm not interested in the prose poem specifically. I wrote a couple— actually I wrote more than a couple but I published only three, I guess: two in a book and one in a magazine. And that was about it.

Why do you think it has been fascinating to a number of people the last ten years?

Partly because it's different from the poem organized by lines. And also, to be candid, I think it's probably easier. And it may be a way of being honest about things. You could divide most of the prose poems I've seen up into lines, and they would look like poems. But it's a modest pleasure to be honest in this way and say, "Well, but that would just be for the show of it, to divide this poem up into lines. I'm just going to put it down here in a natural-looking way and make no pretensions about it." I like that attitude, but I think it's been done enough now so that I'm not interested in it for myself.

Do you think it has been part of, at its best, an experimenting on the frontiers of trying to find out when you cease to write poetry, what poetry can be?

It may well have been for some writers. I don't see it that way as a part of American literary history. It's just another thing that people were doing. I'm not sure that it has very much importance at all. I think it will probably be an occasional thing for your average American poet. I think it should be an option available to anyone. But it has no serious, as far as I can see, no serious importance.

Nor any discovery importance beyond itself?

As far as I can tell, the French discovered it in the middle of the nineteenth century and that was that.

I would be interested in knowing just exactly what you think of emotion in poems, or what you think the place of emotion is or how it works in poems.

I no longer know. At one time I thought I did, and I used to say that I didn't think it had any place in poems, but I'm far less certain about that now. I think probably emotion *does* belong in poetry. But just how much and just where? The question might better be, how to keep it out? I really don't know. As I was saying, I'm much less certain about some things now than I used to be. Someone once told me: "I just gave this poetry reading at a high school (I think it was a high school) and before I was through reading the kids were in tears." And that appalled me. I thought that was, I really thought that was morally wrong. I've never wanted to move people in that physical way through whatever emotion there may be, properly or not, in poetry. I like to think of poems as, ideally, objects of contemplation. Objects, first, of contemplation rather than of action. Action would include the weeping of an audience.

Are not you yourself sometimes moved to tears by poems?

No.

You never have been, by anybody's?

No. And I hope I can say that at the very end as I say it now.

"I never wept." Last words, "I never wept."

Yes. I have been moved close to tears by dramatic occasions, but . . .

You have been moved by poems, emotionally, surely.

Yes, some interior psychological motion, which may have been emotion, yes. But physical evidence was missing.

I'm interested in that. A person can weep inside.

I did come close to weeping many years ago at a play called *A Hatful of Rain* when Shelley Winters picked up the phone and said, "Police, I want to report a junkie," pause, "my husband. . . ." Then the second time I can remember coming close to tears was another dramatic occasion, the movie—what is the name of it?—the movie with Shirley Booth and Burt Lancaster as her alcoholic doctor husband . . .

Come Back, Little Sheba.

Come Back, Little Sheba. And again, by coincidence perhaps, it was when Shirley Booth picked up the phone to call her parents and say something like, "Doc's at it again." And I thought, maybe emotional responses of a gross physical sort were tied for me exclusively to the telephone, and I didn't understand that. I still don't understand it. But those were the first two times in my life since about the age of twelve that I can remember being close to tears. And then last year I saw a performance of a little opera by Hindemith and Thornton Wilder called *The Long Christmas Dinner,* and there was something about the staging of it which moved me very close to tears. The people, when they died, walked down some steps into the audience. They're dying all through the opera, and somehow when they would take that first step down into the audience, some little thing in the corner of my eye would quiver. And I found that so interesting, partly just to observe my own reaction because it was so rare, that I went back to see it the second night it was being performed, and the same thing happened. Every step, practically, boom! Something happened in the corner of my eye. But it's a rare thing, which is one of the reasons I bother to mention it. I am, I hope, stoic.

Do you think poems have an emotional dimension?

Most poetry has what you could call, very simply, content, subject matter—people and events—as novels do. Events like death, love, the death of love, the love of death: I would like to associate the emotion I may be feeling when reading a poem or writing a poem with the event which itself is associated with, or evokes, the emotion. And I do feel the pleasure of recognition or the excitement of being startled that can be aroused by *some* language in *some* poetry now and then, or a sense of admiration or envy, when suddenly a word is very surprising or very revealing, or when a phrase is memorable. I don't know if I'd call that emotion or not. I think of that, in part at least, as an intellectual reaction, which is not quite the same thing, though the two may be tied together.

Well, then you would say of "Absences" that there is an intellectual concept that's behind that?

The poem? I think that the poem is an intellectual construction—as I look at it anyway. But what I refer to throughout that poem is events, rather indirectly sometimes, but events, or people; and emotions are associated with these events, these people.

Well, I don't think it's possible to deal with events or people without the emotional possibilities.

I use a word in that poem that I suppose is loaded with about as much emotion as a word is likely to be for me, the word *palms.* And for me that's a very rich word because of the childhood associations with the palms around where I grew up, and partly it has become richer for me because it now exists *only* in memory—there are no palms in Iowa City—and, furthermore, the palms in Miami happen to be dying. And they always seemed like a really visible physical symbol of—if there is such a thing—something spiritual to me. There is a beauty in palms, I think, perhaps because of childhood associations, and then also because—you know, even this is an intellectual or literary association—Mallarmé uses palms in a beautiful and surprising place in one of his poems, and don't think I didn't think of that when I used the word *palms*, too. But mainly its associations for me are with childhood, as I think is more or less spelled out in the poem.

But it seems to me the poem "Absences" is all about emotion. I mean, it seems to me it is *emotion.*

It's one of the most emotional poems, I guess, I ever wrote. Some people seem to like it, perhaps for that reason.

But I think its content *is emotional and that all of the things you have selected in it, your inclusions, are there because of the emotion that they are adequate to and accurate representations of.*

All right, okay. That seems fair enough to me, yes. I wouldn't have put the cereus in, for instance, if I hadn't felt serious about it. If I may pun. And yet emotion tends to disappear for me, I think, when much show is made of it.

You wouldn't go as far as to say only technique endures? As opposed to Pound's own emotion.

You know, in Pound's work—I don't know it as well as many people do—but it seems to me that his technique may well last at least as long as the emotion. Anyway, with some poets, it might be that the technique is indeed what endures. And I don't think that's a judgment involving value or hierarchies. A normal reaction might be to think, oh yes, those whose technique only endures are the lesser poets. I'm not sure that's the case.

But isn't technique at the service of something? Almost by definition— I wouldn't say almost—*in* fact *by definition.*

Well, maybe so.

Technique, the practice of doing something.

Maybe so.

Well, let's go back to "the impulse to poetry." What is the technique at the service of? Recording fact or moment? Rescuing from oblivion? Embodying the emotional reality of an experience? Consider your poem "Landscape with Little Figures." That poem would seem to be a good example of your sense of enriching the content of a poem by leaving out. But actually what is left out of that poem is still completely apprehensible in the emotional aura of a time and a place—and even, one assumes, of your life.

Yes, that's good, if you get that sense from it.

But why is that good?

Well, because it . . . Let me try to say this right. It is good (if it is) because it had to be through the verbal construction rather than the facts of experience that it came to seem so, and therefore the purpose of the poem, or one of the purposes of the poem, reaches its end, is successful in that way, in that it does something of what it set out to do. I think it does that by equivalence, though that's not a very clear way of putting it, but I think it operates—as many poems do—like this: I go through these emotions in the poem and thereby you see, yes, it *is* as if such and such *were* so, or as if such and such were to be felt. I don't think the correspondence between what is felt or seen by a reader can possibly be the same as what I first knew, but I have, as it were, mediated between the reader and what could be known only to me by way of these lines, these words and phrases. Partly to conceal, really, rather than to reveal. I'm talking about A in the poem, say, and in truth I'm thinking B. But I'm talking about A so that *you* can feel or see C. That's too complicated a way to try for such a simple little point, but . . .

It's kind of poetry by deflection.

That's a better way of putting it, a simpler way. I'm not really talking straight in that poem—even in that poem, simple and childlike as it may seem.

I'm too dense to understand what you mean by that. I don't understand what you mean when you say that the emotion was excluded. I don't understand.

I haven't looked at that poem in a long time, but I think I remember it.

I want to read it to you.

Well, no, I think I remember it well enough to know that it pretends to be talking about the change that took place in a certain neighborhood, and it . . .

I think it is talking about that.

Yes, OK. That's its ostensible subject matter, that's the vehicle for the emotion. And the place, this neighborhood, has changed, sadly. Things are not as they were. And I think that's a kind of image for a secret subject which I don't announce in the poem. And don't intend to announce now.

Don't you think that all poems do that?

Yes. A lot of poems *are* like that.

But isn't the point that the emotion appropriate to the one you do not directly announce is also the emotion that you endow that "as if" thing with? In other words, that emotion is present. You simply use another vehicle to express that . . .

OK. Yes. I think all this we're saying is really what I was trying to get at with my elaborate A B C's.

But my point is that that emotion is not excluded in any sense, and it is not denied. A moment, a particular example of it from your private experience, is perhaps not rendered as the vehicle for us to apprehend, true . . .

Yes, that may be unimportant. That's true. But I would like to insist that my own private view of it *is* left out, whether it matters that it's left out or not. Although I do know where the neighborhood was, you know. I'm using something true to fake with. And you can't see it there anymore, you know. That's true, too.

But don't you think anyone who would read that poem would know it's not about a neighborhood? Anyone who's sophisticated enough to read . . .

Maybe so, maybe I'm just simple-minded about my own work. I'm not trying to be funny. But I always thought if I said, say, Rivershore Drive, people would think I meant Rivershore Drive, whereas I felt that I had preserved a secret since I really didn't mean Rivershore Drive. Apparently people must have been reading me all along and knowing that I didn't mean anything like Rivershore Drive.

What I'm wanting to suggest, really, finally, through my posing of questions on this is, tentatively, that the real subject matter of this poem (as, maybe, in many other poems of yours and other people), is that emotion.

You may be right.

Not another *thing . . .*

You may be right, but I would feel obliged to maintain that insofar as that was true I was unaware of it. I thought I was dealing with other materials. That is, I thought I was dealing with the raw materials of language and rhythm. Usually, when I'm working with a poem, it is such matters as those that I am consciously thinking of. Of choosing among a hoard of words, adjusting rhythms, little things like that.

But you choose for feel, too, don't you?

Probably I would tend to choose, ordinarily, a word richer in what could conveniently be called emotional association than a word poorer, though I've made other choices, words poor in association, on purpose. So it's not always the one thing. But that is, at least, what my conscious mind, when I'm working on a poem, is dealing with. Just the simple raw materials of language and rhythm. I think most words you use in poetry are unavoidably full of content, and so you're dealing with content, too. But that, for me, has always seemed secondary. Now I may be fooling myself.

Do you think there can be any difference between content and subject matter?

No, no, I meant only subject matter, content, whatever term is used. You see, all I want to claim is that, for me, in the process of working, what my conscious mind was attending to was something other than the subject matter, at least primarily. And I'm not trying to boast that it was so or apologize for the fact that it was so, just to describe the case.

Don't you think that's inevitable? That if, in fact, you knew what it was, you couldn't write it or couldn't deal with it or you wouldn't want to, that it would be solved?

For me, that is so.

I think that's certainly true for me, too.

It is? Well, I'm glad to hear it. You know, sometimes it's good to exchange one's sense of things with other people because— don't you ever have the feeling that you're the only one who is tilted in that particular way?

Exactly, oh, yes. But I think we're all tilted in that way. Still, to pursue this point, it does seem to me that that's what the poem is groping toward and after, and that whatever else you're doing, all the skill that you're bringing to bear is, finally, to enable that subject matter to find a local habitation, a home.

You know, ever since I mentioned the word *photograph* earlier, just casually—I had never thought of it that way before—I've been thinking in the back of my mind that it would be a pleasure to write a series of poems which simulated photographs, which really did make up a little album. I don't know. I realized as soon as I said the word some minutes ago that probably none of my poems resembled photographs at all and maybe it would be good to be more direct about it instead of roundabout, and, I don't know, maybe I'll try to write some of those.

Let me ask you this question, not in any reductive way at all! I'd like it to kind of open out and see how willing you would be to go a little farther with it. Robert Bly said somewhere, sometime, something to the effect that American poets are too concerned with form, or have been too concerned with form, historically. Now, leaving Robert Bly aside, what do you think of that? As, not only a poet but as a teacher of poets, a conductor of workshops, much involved at the center of the development of American poetry and as an observer of American poetry: what do you think of that?

I think it's partly true and partly not true. It's an exaggeration, it's a propaganda point. There have been brief periods in American literary history, I'm sure, when there has been too much absorption with obvious form. And then—since you did mention Bly as a source for the opinion—one of the times when that was probably true was when he was maturing, as it was of the time when I was maturing. Same period.

Well, I think maybe he said "technique." Excuse me.

Or technique, yes. Things probably do move (later they seem to have moved, when you look back at them) in terms of reactions to what came just before. Another commonplace. And if around 1950 most poets were writing in quatrains, say, it would be natural as a historical process, as a literary process, to stop writing quatrains after a while and to say we were writing too many quatrains, or paying too much attention to technique or to form—whatever term one chose—and to go in another direction. To keep changing—that's probably healthy in the literary life of a culture, as I *definitely* believe it is healthy in the life of a person to keep changing. I'm unsatisfied with the work of most poets who early found a formula and then reproduced it over and over. And I think it would be a sign of deadening in the culture of a nation if a formula were found and simply articulated thereafter into eternity. You know things are going to change. So I think if that were said specifically of twenty years ago he would have to be right; if he were speaking of, say, 1970, he would be wrong. That's all there is to it. Poets were *not*, in 1970, too much concerned with form.

I think I sense in that a certain dissatisfaction with an insufficient attention to technique. Am I right?

Yes. Or else . . .

That you think, in other words, that it has gone too far the other way, the reaction.

Yes, I think the time will come, may even now be upon us, for a healthy reaction in the other direction, perhaps not ever to the extent that we experienced right after the war. Literary fashions! The changing generations! It's funny to have watched so much of it, both from the sidelines and as a player of the game. Nostalgic, like watching old movies. There are several poems in *Departures* which sort of twit the younger generation and the older lookers-on as well—a little double-sided. "The Telephone Number of the Muse" means to operate both ways. The last lines of "Self-Portrait as Still Life" announce my position on that, if I have one. Probably, you know, with experience, it begins to seem that nobody has *all* the right of it. There are things to be said on too many sides.

What has been gained by American poetry in, say, the reaction against the extreme formalism of the fifties? What's been gained?

Certain things are obvious. A broadening of subject matter, for one thing, which is a curious accompaniment to the destruction of form. An opening up of subject matter, I believe. And also more fluency. The syntax of poetry being written in 1950, to take the same exemplary year, the syntax tended to be self-conscious, convoluted, elaborate, restrictive, though sometimes the poems were indeed interesting compositions. Now poets can, it seems to me, be more fluent, easy-going, natural, can say more things. I'm trying to speak of what seem to be virtues. I think a vice that's arisen—oh, there are several obvious vices, no doubt—is so great a lack of formal awareness or concern that an unattractive, an actively unpleasant, chaos results, a total abandonment of what I would call, very simply, organization. Order, to be more high-toned. And this, then, is not only absent but prized for being absent, which I cannot go along with. And also—to use a popular term these days—a certain type of "inwardness." Inwardness may be fine for some, but it really can be a drag to others, including me. I mean, I am at least as interested in plain fact as I am in the mystical speculations of X, Y, and Z. And there has been a great *outpouring* of inwardness, and of a sort that almost always goes in the direction of the mystical. And none of that really is at all interesting to me. Against fashion, I know, but there has been a great deal more self-indulgence of that kind in the poetry of 1970 than in the poetry of 1950. So it seems things balance out. Some good, some not so good.

Do you think as a part of that fluency that poets are able to write a more American language and rhythm?

That's probably true. Some poets were already able to. But more poets prize it now than formerly, and that is a gain, if we are to think in evolutionary terms.

Is it possible to write an American line, an American diction, an American language, in toto, in traditional forms?

Obviously, since it was done by Robert Frost, for one. He didn't always do it, but, my God, he did it in so many lines that to imagine that it's impossible seems to me ridiculous, if you can read and if you can hear. Sure, Robert Frost did it. Not many others have done it, not so often, so aptly and so expressively. I wouldn't want to sound like Robert Frost in many of my poems. Who would? But he certainly did *that*. If that's the assigned task, he completed it successfully. . . .

You say in the note in Departures *that certain of the poems come, in part, from chance methods. What do you mean by that?*

Well, first as to the "in part." Those, I believe, who really commit themselves to chance in the various arts would go all the way and let chance govern. So, the "in part" is meant to say that I only go so far with it, or that I'm not really a Cage, obviously enough; I like elegance, as he once told me, and the Cage methods do not necessarily result in elegance. But I was interested in finding a further means of keeping myself distant. I thought it would be interesting to simulate a small computer without actually using one, and so I wrote words onto a great number of note cards, words which I had taken from passages of poems I admired. My own taste, in other words, was involved in the preparations, so that I might think of whatever result was to come as mine, somewhat mine. Thus the "in part": not surrendering totally to the gods of chance. If I were doing that, I could simply open a book, any book, and just take the words down. I can see I haven't explained this very clearly. Anyway, here is what I went through in trying to get in touch with chance: I wrote down on note cards a lot of words from poems I liked. I chose a good number of sentences which interested me as sentences, as syntactical forms, and I wrote these down on another set of note cards. I divided the word cards up into three groups, nouns, verbs, and adjectives, from which I thought I could generate any other parts of speech necessary to deal with the sentences. I then shuffled the sentence cards, as I called them, and dealt myself a sentence, you might say, and where the sentence called for a noun, I shuffled the noun cards and dealt myself a noun. And where it called for a verb, the same. And so on. I found in working around with this that chance wasn't all that good to me the first time through, so on some large sheets of paper I tried filling in each sentence three times. Then I would have what seemed a multitude of choices, but actually a workable limit, and having three words to choose from in each place in each sentence meant that I could generate a number of sentences from each sentence card, and I could go on for as many sentences as I wanted to. By then I might have quite a few lines and I found that when things were going well, when I was being dealt winning hands, so to speak, the sentences seemed to cohere to some degree; and where they cohered to a lesser degree than I approved of, I was willing to violate chance and impose myself, to make connections or to leave things out. The first few times I tried it I was running a hot streak, and I thought that I had found a way to write poems forever, one I could give to friends even, but now, well . . . well, I'm not all that much . . .

Only your closest *friends.*

Yes. I'm not all that much for increasing the world's population of poems, so I guess I would have restricted it to a few. But then the more I tried it the less productive it became. I had made my first set of cards in Syracuse and after exhausting that first set I made up another out in California. And that second set exhausted itself much more quickly than the first, so I haven't tried it a third time. Anyway, I realized fairly soon that it wasn't the solution to the problem of writing poems. But I like some of the results and in any case I would only keep whatever results seemed true and not just lucky. I wasn't going to give myself totally to chance. I wanted esthetic choice. I reserved the right to do my own work. But it did seem to me to simulate the actual working of the imagination.

I mean, one does have an accumulated store of words and some notions of what interesting sentences would be like; and with this process you didn't have to wait, didn't have to do that dull sort of beginning work, or you did it in a different way, so that it seemed stimulating and interesting. And I certainly must have come up with some lines and some images that I would never have gotten otherwise even with the very hardest work. For a little while there I felt I could say to the gods that don't exist, "Give me a poem," and they would respond.

(1975)

An Interview with Paul Ruffin

I want to get into your craft a little bit. Richard Howard notes that the one special quality of your poetry is its "elegance," an elegance which derives from "a special accommodation of the poem's shape and body to its impulse or 'message' until nothing remains outside the form, left over to be said in any way except *by the poem itself." Could you comment on this observation?*

As far as I can and do believe, that is the description of an ideal poem; and so far as I don't believe that my poems are ideal, it doesn't seem to me anything except *hopeful* as a description of my own work. I would like for poems to manage to do that regularly, or more or less regularly, but I don't really think they do. It seems to me there's always something not said or not said expressively, and there is often too *much* said.

If you had to choose—and thank Providence poets do not, except in interviews—between form and content, which would you consider to be the, oh, the more important in poetic composition?

It's a good thing you added "in poetic composition." In life content is more important, and in art, I think, form is more important. Insofar as they are distinct. And I believe it is possible to see that there are some differences, despite the bent of critical opinion. In life I don't care much about form, and in art I care a good deal about it. But form cannot prevent content from entering, unless one is writing nonsense, and content hardly gets in without some form; so there's a reciprocity. But poetry is an art which has traditionally encouraged the appearance of form which can be apprehended.

Would you consider yourself a formalist, a traditionalist, in poetry?

Yes.

In an essay on Karl Shapiro's The Bourgeois Poet *you suggested that you liked best those parts that were at the same time "wildest and most formal." You called that "surely a winning combination." There seems to be a paradox here.*

It's an obvious one, isn't it? I think that a passage or a poem that seemed openly formal might seem patently dull if it had only the tamest, most conventional, predictable matter appearing in it. One of the obvious means for countering that possibility is to put into it material with a certain strangeness, unexpectedness, even—if you like—wildness. Baudelaire is a fine example within the tradition of a poet whose work generally has a high degree of formal sophistication and accomplishment while containing matter of a certain strangeness and, in some cases, wildness. The two make together what critics from the beginning were willing to describe as a *frisson*. That's one thing I would wish to happen, too, in poems. So I would subscribe to what I said then: I think it's a winning formula if the two can be brought together.

Is that what you attempt to do in your poetry?

I don't think I'm quite that conscious of it. That's what I would like to plan to do when I can. You can't always summon up "wildness," and you can't always count on formal excellence. There might well be some distance between desire and accomplishment. I can't think offhand of ever trying deliberately to introduce wild notes, but if they come up as a part of the sweep of the subject, then it's fine with me—I'd like to make room for them.

Would you mind giving me an example of a poem of yours that achieves that balance, whether deliberately or subconsciously?

I think several of them do. By relative measures the wildest thing of mine might seem quite tame to others. A poem called "The Assassination" is an example. If the essential *wildness* of that is not seen, well . . .

You've studied under a number of very well-known poets, including Yvor Winters, Karl Shapiro, Robert Lowell, and John Berryman. Who of these appears to have been the dominant influence in your poetic theory, in your finished poems?

That's a rather special way of asking the question. To try to answer that specific question, I will say probably Winters, because I had read his criticism and met him and sat in classes of his before I met and listened to the others. On the other hand, the teacher I thought was the most responsible and responsive and interesting and interested within the classroom itself was John Berryman. That's an answer to a different question.

Your early background was Southern: birth in Florida, south Georgia family history, some years in North Carolina. Has the South manifested itself a great deal in your poetry?

In some of the poems I wrote before any of those collected in the books, yes, but that would be invisible to others; and in some of the poems in *Summer Anniversaries;* and unavoidably, I suppose, in some cast of mind or inflection of speech or the way of noting or not noting details. One fairly recent poem is Southern in that it deals with a Southern experience. But I don't think I'm a Southern poet, and I don't think I *was* for very long. I'm Southern only by fact of birth and growing up.* No, I'm not self-consciously regional. I don't *talk* with much of a Southern accent anymore.

No, you don't.

If I do at all today, it's probably because of this cold.

I don't think you do at all.

On the other hand, I didn't consciously eschew talking Southern: I just lived elsewhere long enough.

Do you think that had you stayed in the South your art would have taken a different course?

Inevitably. I do think that where you live and whom you talk to and what you do have a great deal to do with what you write.

Would your poetry have been better?

Maybe.

So you don't really consider yourself a Southern poet at all?

No. In fact, there are a couple of poems in *Summer Anniversaries* that may seem to have Southern sympathies which are actually good-byes to the South. "Beyond the Hunting Woods" means to say just that by implication, for example. It means to say good-bye at least to the *myths* of the old South.

Oh yeah, but that heavy nostalgia seems to be directly from a Southern poet who's not about to leave the region.

Well, you see, I read heavily in the Fugitives, the Agrarians, and my thinking for a short period was much influenced by

---

*In 1982 I moved back to Florida.

them. Then it became possible to lift my eyes up and look around me at what was actually there and to remember my own past and what I had heard of my family's past and to realize that all that I had been reading about seemed a kind of mythmaking that had absolutely no relevance to the social facts as I knew them. So it seemed to me like a literary phenomenon rather than a phenomenon of life. There were certainly no Confederate generals in *my* background: there were dirt farmers, sharecroppers, and the like. That was the South I could see and knew and the South that was suffering and being. So I began—while respecting the writing of Ransom, Tate, and Warren—less and less to believe that the dreams of past glory meant a damned thing anymore. Certainly not to me.

(1977)

An Interview with Larry Levis

How did you begin writing? Do you remember exactly?

Not exactly. It was during adolescence, when many people must start. I think there is a sort of stir, a boiling up of things. What I was really interested in was writing music—I had a kind of basic artistic . . . desire. At the same time, I read a lot. Reading a lot, playing a lot of music and trying to write music, I began to write a few other things, little stories and poems. Most of this was done in isolation. My friends were often musicians and one of them also wanted to write music. And yet I knew no one who wanted to write stories or poems. So what writing I did was done in even greater isolation until, I suppose, I got to college, at which time I began to think more seriously about it, and met a few others who had similar ambitions. But it was a long time, quite a few years, before I began to settle on poetry rather than prose.

Do you think that playing, or practicing music, influenced you as a poet, or would it be possible to know whether it did?

It must have, but in what specific ways I can't imagine. One of the dimensions of poetry that have always fascinated me has been the rhythms, the meters, and I suppose that would be roughly analogous to something in music—but the rhythms of music and of poetry are by no means the same. There would be a common sensibility in composing music and writing poems; the same sort of . . . of creative desire would obviously lie behind virtually any of the arts. But music and poetry are the two that I know most about from personal experience. In both there is the same kind of joy in working something out, quite compulsively perhaps, and that is what must have engaged me when I tried to write music, and does now when I try to work out a poem. The joy of working it out and completing it are both part of the process of making something up—I don't mean inventing only but actually creating something—and then trying to get it right.

Do you think that translating, say translating Eugène Guillevic, and other poets, has had much effect on your own work?

Reading what was then contemporary French poetry in the early sixties, as I was doing for a project—getting together a book of French translations—reading in that poetry did affect what I was writing . . . and especially when I found a poet who seemed to have a singular style *unmatched* by any of the styles then or now in vogue in American poetry—Guillevic. Just to read him seemed to constitute a kind of discovery for me. I had, for a while, the ambition to translate that *style*, as it were, into American verse. That was a passing interest, but it did engage me seriously for a while and I think that I did manage to do just that, in fact, but it made no difference to anybody else, as far as I could tell, or to the history of poetry. . . . I'm glad I did it. What I tried to do, once I found a style in another language which was to me of great interest, was to put it into American. My interest apparently wasn't shared, and, having done it, I wasn't interested in continuing. It wasn't really my style, anyway, just *a* style. So . . . I don't do that anymore. When, a little later, Denise Levertov translated Guillevic, she translated him better than most poets get translated. But her translations did not seem to me much interested in achieving a style in American that would be distinct from what she and her friends had already written.

She seemed, in a way, interested in his vision, in his social vision.

Yes, which was a matter of considerable concern. I was interested in it, too. But once the poetry of Guillevic had been defined in that way for an American reading public, I felt that a purer interest in the style as style was less to the point.

Since you teach here at the University of Iowa's Writers' Workshop, would you care to mention any of those things you might want to warn a young poet against? Or, what advice might you have for a young poet today?

I really should have ready answers to that question, I'm sure. But I don't. Let me try to account for that. . . . One of my theories or principles has been, rightly or wrongly, to try to avoid imposing a set of prescriptions on students. I used to believe in that position strongly, but in the last few years my sense of the rightness of that view has begun to crumble away. So I don't know. If in three or four years I am still teaching, I might start giving very specific warnings, very explicit advice. I've always wanted to try to deal with the work they were already doing, try to see what the potential power and direction of that work was and try to strengthen it in its own way or push it along its own path. That's merely an ideal. I've never been able to succeed in doing that, but that at least has been my theory of teaching young writers. As I say, I've begun to despair of that position lately, and I don't know quite where I stand now on this. Clearly there are certain easy things one can say: Don't overwrite, for instance. Or practical advice like: Do consider revision. Simple things like that. Which some people are unprepared to hear, or to act on, simple and obvious though they are. Another thing that has begun to bother me and which I would like to warn people of, if I believed it was right to generalize, would be simply: Don't write like those others. I mean: Don't write like everyone else here. Also: Don't write like those poets whom everybody has agreed to admire. More and more I think of such exemplars as Pound—not that I like everything he wrote—but one of the things he did, and with the courage of the young and self-confident, was to go out and piece together a new culture for himself. That was a good part of his originality, I think. Now I seem to observe among the people here, including the best young writers, that somehow by the time they arrive here as graduate students, even though they come from various parts of the country, they all know who the six good poets are in the country. Usually, of course, these six don't happen to be the six *I* think are good. But there seems to be a common consent, and they all wish, apparently, to write like these half-dozen. I think that is a mistake, I really do. But what is one to do? Play the dictator? I know I'm tired of hearing the prescriptions others so willingly and, indeed, loudly offer. So I'm not sure yet that it would be right to say: Don't write like X; don't write like Y. For one thing, actually to write like X, even though X might be a terrible poet, might work out well for . . . for Z. I just don't think there is any knowing about these things. I do like to say, over and over in class: Try to be clear. But such matters are more like universal, historical principles . . .

Do you foresee yourself in the next few years writing, as you have been lately, in more traditional forms? I am thinking, for example, of your poem "Childhood," which used a relaxed blank verse, or of "First Death," a poem in rhymed octosyllabic couplets.

Yes, I think I will write more formal verse, or continue to write somewhat more formal verse, by and large. It is more difficult and more challenging for me. I would like the art not to be lost, either by me personally or by the world at large. A student said to me the other day, "But nobody writes that kind of stuff anymore." Many people must think that. Therefore it becomes a matter of honor to try it. To do so is in its way . . . well, rebellion is too strong a term . . . but a pulling against the tide.

Which might be fun.

Yes. Part of the pleasure of writing in a traditional meter is the kind of simple pleasure you get in solving problems. You set yourself a problem, and you solve it. Writing almost always has something of that in it but in this way a part of your brain can become involved with an almost irrelevant problem while the rest of it is occupied with what's generally conceded to be important—without overconcentration or hysteria.

Or confronting something head-on, and therefore, maybe, making it impossible.

Yes, right.

You know, a kind of sixties' notion about surrealism seemed to suggest that one could just simply plunge in, and face the unconscious.

Well, it's worth a try, but you don't always come up with treasure.

It seemed to me, as a poet growing up in the 1960s, that it was a decade relatively free of any kind of criticism of contemporary poetry, and in fact I really didn't feel that it had much place then, or perhaps that it didn't want much place in talking about contemporary poetry, and certainly the poets didn't seem to want any advice, at that point. Now, it seems to me that things have shifted in a way that I certainly couldn't have foreseen, say, in 1969, and the critic has become important again. I don't want to mention names, but it seems impossible to exclude the name of Harold Bloom from the resurrection of that kind of . . .

There is a joke abroad about his tastes in contemporary work: someday he'll get beyond the A's.

Yes, I've heard that one. And since Ammons and Ashbery are two of his favorite living poets . . .

Well, but what you say is true. There's no argument about that. . . . And I myself feel now, looking back, the loss of an intelligent, perceptive, powerful criticism accompanying the production of new work. The absence wasn't actually felt and experienced during the sixties. In fact, as I remember it, there was some rejoicing over the decline of criticism. But now it can be seen as an absence or loss, just as you say. The criticism we have now, as far as I can tell, is by no means of the same class as, say, the criticism that was flourishing in the forties, when I began to read and write.

So you would have had, then, say . . . Blackmur?

Yes, Blackmur is a wonderful example, and Tate, and Ransom, and, for me, Winters. Well, practically anyone who wrote poetry also wrote criticism. . . . Jarrell began to; Lowell did very good reviews from time to time. It was just taken as part of the job of the "man of letters." But it really did change. I guess poets now are writing a little criticism again, but I must have been reading the wrong journals, because I haven't seen much that is good. In fact, I haven't seen much that has the basic virtue of being exact, or that even wishes to be exact. I've seen a good deal of vague praise, and vague, sometimes sneering criticism of new work . . .

In the nature of a book review . . . ?

Yes, but there is a kind of criticism that I have begun to associate with *The American Poetry Review* which, well . . . it has a style, but the substance I don't understand. And I really don't think that if something is *clearly said* I would fail to understand it. I have confidence in my own ability to read and understand the language. I can understand the spirit of the piece and sometimes the poems that are being written about or the principles involved, but I do not understand how what is being said can be applied to the examples offered, at least not in the way I have always understood literary criticism and philosophy to work—the same remarks can apply to *any* of the poems, and of course that's not right. Perhaps criticism is in danger of becoming too much an art in itself, detached—or too much a personal or intellectual word-game, as they used to say poetry was, wrongly. In any case, criticism now seems very different.

How might that be? I sense what you're saying there, but it seems to me, at least in the texts I've read, there is a kind of diffuseness that I would never have found in, say, the New Critics. I don't know whether that arose because, in the sixties, the New Critics were being disparaged, and people wanted to find a criticism that was "relevant." Therefore, they would search outside the given field, and come back from a perspective, *like Structuralism . . .*

I don't know. . . . That's a large way of looking at it, and it's probably quite valid. But because of the nature of my university experience (I've taught in workshops for years) I make an association, on a much smaller scale, with the kind of criticism one encounters in workshops. A lot of the people who would write for a journal like *The American Poetry Review* are the graduates or victims of workshops, and though this may have no historical validity at all, it seems to me the kind of pretentious and dogmatic vapidity I find in some pieces in such places. . . . I also hear it as criticism in workshops and have heard it for years. In a workshop you can sometimes ask the person who is saying such things to stop a moment and reflect, but there is no stopping the flow of critical prose one finds in articles and many reviews.

Another thing I find in the criticism you do get now, in fact the very kind of thing workshops *sponsor*, because of their nature, is a rush to judgment. The opinion is arrived at before the poem is considered, you might say. I remember a famous poet once visiting a meeting of the workshop and looking at the poems on the worksheet and being able to tell instantly that she liked the poems best which had small letters at the beginnings of the lines. It was like a reflex action: before the poem had been read it was possible to make a judgment on it—because certain signs were present. And it seems to me that probably most of us in the poetry "world" now have memorized the signs by which we know, immediately, how we're going to react to the text we haven't yet looked at. I'm sure I've done this at times, but I think it's terrible, and I think that's part of the problem—I know this doesn't amount to a very rational analysis of contemporary criticism, but one note of hope might be that people are getting involved with criticism again, trying to find things they can actually say about the work they are reading and presumably talking about, and if so that would be an improvement.

Well, I can think of a couple of good examples lately in that large issue of Antaeus *(nos. 30–31) devoted to poetry and poetics—your remarks on meter, and also an article by Robert Hass which spoke to the problem of form, and which suggested some sort of return to a more traditional mode.*

That's my own inclination, of course. But I would be interested, too—well, maybe this is a contradiction in terms—in responsible experiment. That isn't quite what I mean. In experiment which was, in itself, quite exciting, new, and, let us say, not too tendentious or theoretical.

Tendentious in terms of experiments that have already gone on, or . . . ?

Yes. Or experiments in the service of some ill-defined theory. There is an excitement still in reading . . . to me there is . . . in reading Williams' poems from the early twenties. The poems still seem to me to contain the thrill of discovery, and actually there may be something equally interesting happening now. But I haven't noticed it in magazines or books. I may just not have been lucky enough to come across it. Something like that, what Williams did . . . in fact, I think *that* is tradition, too. I would like to include all that *in* tradition.

One question occurred to me the other day, which might have something to do with what we're talking about, although I guess the experiment wouldn't necessarily be formal—but an experiment in terms of subject matter, or content. I was reading a short story by a man named Randall Reid, in an old issue of the New American Review, *and it was suddenly clear to me—I was about to go in to teach a workshop, and what seemed clear to me was that the fiction writer could include so many* more *kinds of experience, and drastically different experi-*

ences. In other words, a novelist or short story writer could create a totally immoral narrator, in the first person, which I have not seen done, really, in poetry lately, except in persona poems—which have taken on a kind of flowering, I guess, although they still seem curiously bound by a, well . . . usually by an historical or literary character—and sometimes the poems are astonishingly good. But suddenly I was aware of . . . almost when you start to write a poem, at least if you use an "I" voice, you respond, or I feel that I sometimes respond, to poetry itself. That may be unavoidable.

Well, yes. There's a whole bundle of opinions about poetry abroad now in the part of our culture that *notices* poetry at all, and one is that *Poetry is good for you,* to put it into the simplest possible terms. And mostly when we sit down to write poetry we're expected to be writing poems that are going to be "good" for us and "good" for other people, too. Some such attitude undoubtedly lies behind the Poetry-in-the-Schools program, for instance. Now a novelist doesn't have to think of anything like that, and that's obviously an advantage for the novelist. But in poetry you're expected to say certain things— for instance, the one I use as an example of this sort of thing—you're expected to say that *Nature is good.* If you don't, your view is taken to be anti-poetical. Or you're expected to say—this is a little less common, but it's very prevalent— you're expected to say that government is *bad.* Both of those propositions may be true, but if you're a poet you're expected to share this sort of . . . reflex view and that seems to me to put an excessive restriction on the individual personality of the poet. To mention Pound again, although I really do think his politics, so far as I became acquainted with them, were nutty and reprehensible . . . he didn't go along with that sort of Ladies' Club view of poetry. What is astonishing to me is that intelligent, sophisticated friends of mine who are gifted poets, who write well, seem to me to share, pretty much, a Ladies' Club notion of what poetry is: it's *good for the Soul*— they act as if they believed there were something almost sacred in the name of *poet.* Maybe there was, in primitive societies . . . but I think that has all been shorn away, for better or for worse, from our calling. I think it's a very honorable calling, but I don't want to make any special claims for it in the world at large. Art is for me virtually the greatest thing in experience, but unless you already know that and believe it, I don't want to sell that view to you; I don't want to make false claims to the wrong people. But look—nowadays the poet is expected to be of a certain type and to hold certain predetermined views—by expressing these attitudes, for instance, you can always get approval from an audience at a poetry reading. This is a vague response to what you were saying, but I think it's connected.

I think it is, yes. It struck me once—I was writing an elegy—that there were certain things about an elegy that existed . . . as rules.

OK, conventions. Sometimes, though, conventions are liberating because you don't have to think about the way you're going to resolve a problem. Not everything has to be invented anew at each occasion. But when you've *got to do it* according to prescription, it rubs you the wrong way.

Well, yes, if only because it feels like a curious kind of precensorship.

That's right. One of the reasons I guess I responded to your question this way—you were suggesting that the story presented an amoral point-of-view character and . . . well, we certainly have enough amoral poets running around, but in their poems they often come through as the nicest people you could want to meet, with all the correct poetic attitudes, which is understandable. I mean, anybody can present himself or herself as he or she wishes, but it is funny that we don't feel free to be . . . *mean* in poetry as much as we do, say, in criticism.

Yes, of course a fiction writer can always absolve himself by saying, "Of course it's not me . . ." But maybe there is a special way in which people who read you as a poet think they're really getting you.

Actually, I would like to keep that true. When I say *I* in a poem, I would like to be saying what I really do think and believe and have done or seen or experienced. But I would like also to have available to me the possibility of writing a narrative or dramatic poem, in which there would be characters and everybody would know they were characters, or I would be inventing a story, and everyone would know I was inventing a story. One of the curious things that have happened in what . . . the last five, six years particularly, or maybe it goes back further, but I've noticed it in the last years more than ever before, and I think you mentioned this earlier, in speaking of persona poems—the character of the writer and the character or characters in the poems get mixed up somehow, and I can no longer make the historical and conventional distinctions which seem so important to me. This may represent an advance in the art, but in the meantime I'm puzzled . . . I don't quite see it . . . I mean, in Browning's "The Bishop Orders His Tomb . . ." no one can suppose that's really Browning. Browning has a great interest in the Renaissance and knows a lot about it, and he has a certain attitude toward the worldliness and luxuries the Church indulged in, and so on. Yet you know, clearly and definitely, it's not Browning talking, and the poem is the better for that. Now, if some of our poets were to write about a bishop ordering a tomb, you might think: My lord, I hadn't known he was a bishop! You know, there might be a sort of unacknowledged confusion of a poet with narrator, an assumption perhaps by the poet not only of the narrator's voice and personality but of his very history. The poet as incubus! A dissolution of genre, I think has occurred, and it fascinates a lot of young writers, but it also seems to be a way which makes it, well, to be quite frank, awfully easy to write, or at least makes it possible to write interestingly without having done very much or thought very much. I am of about three minds on this score. I don't *think* I like it; on the other hand, I'm not sure.

I feel that I do like some of it. I mean, when it works it seems to be the Other's experience, or the experience of the persona has meant so much to the poet that he is speaking through *it.*

Aren't you surprised at how easy it seems to be to assimilate a great multitude and variety of experience which others have spared us the necessity of acquiring for ourselves, and not only to assimilate but to write about . . . I mean, if you develop, as a lot of people seem to have done during the last few years, a great affection for Chekhov, say . . . then you can invent for yourself Chekhovian characters and situations or even borrow passages from things he wrote and treat them as if they were your own, almost your own. I cannot believe that if you feel that way about Chekhov you could feel that way about a hundred others, too, and master their experience as well simply by turning the pages.

No, I don't think you could do that, or at least it might begin to look . . . suspect.

Maybe you *can,* actually . . . I don't know, but it just doesn't seem possible to *me.* Picasso assimilated the experience of generations of other painters. He seemed to have an all-encompassing, an "all-gathering-in," character as an artist. But there aren't many like that. Stravinsky had a similar capacity; nevertheless in his life, even more than in Picasso's, his work could be divided, it did divide, into periods—for a while he was a Neo-Classicist, and did everything you can do in that respect; later he became a serial composer, too, and before either he'd been a primitive, a very sophisticated primitive. But it wasn't as if in 1928, say, he was doing *all* these things at once, being a Russian folklorist and Pergolesi and a Webernite at the same time.

Yes, right. Of course, it could be, too, that the poetry you're talking about here is in part a reaction to an earlier poetry, the poetry of the sixties, that centered itself so often and so solidly on the "I." People may have felt a need to get away, to get out from under that.

Oh, yes, that's probably true historically. What we may need, in criticism, is a lot of good, careful, exact criticism for a few years until things get shaken and sorted out and settled down again and we know where we are. So that we can go on from there, and take off again. I really don't know where we are at the moment. I have a hard enough time just knowing where *I* am, and where everybody else is seems to me quite mysterious. Ten years ago, I could have generalized more easily. It may be interesting not to know, but I wish somebody would tell me where everything belongs.

I don't know if anybody could.

Well, that's what criticism might do. Not so much tell us what we should be writing tomorrow as show us how to think well and clearly about what we have just written.

Which is what it did, *say, in the 1940s.*

I think so. At least Eliot's criticism, for example, showed you what he had mastered in order to write what he was writing. And that was very valuable, I think.

And beyond that, even in his earliest essays, he was so eloquent that he was kind of irresistible. Another question: When you write, whom do you write for? Do you have anyone in mind? I was thinking of Berryman, who was asked that question once, and he said: "Well, I write for about fifteen people," and there was this pause, and he said: "Thirty, if you count their wives."

Or husbands!

Or husbands, *sure.*

That's a funny remark. Well, I remember the first time I was ever asked that question, and my answer was "Dick Stern," who was my best and truest reader back then—that was quite a while ago. It's harder to answer, now, but . . . well . . . almost always it would be for Milton's "fit audience but few." Though you naturally hope that others would read some of what you write with understanding and pleasure. *I* think that, first of all, I write for myself. I know that's an obvious answer, but I'm the first person who sees the work, and the first person who is either satisfied or bothered by it. Then, as I have got older, I have seen that I would like to be writing also for the future . . . because I have observed how great is the time lag between the writing of a piece and the time when other people have a chance to see it. By the time that happens, it already seems old to me. You must have had the same feeling, and we just have to get used to that if we can. Someone will say to me that he just saw such and such a poem of mine and liked it. Fine—but someone said that to me a couple of weeks ago, and I remembered I had written the poem in 1954. I had to be pleased that the poem had lasted twenty-five years, but I would rather for my reader to have seen a poem I had just written, and felt the same way about that. There are at least those two ways of looking at it. It's good to know that something has hung on for a little while, but it would also be good to get a more immediate response. That's almost impossible, except with, say, Berryman's fifteen friends, and, possibly, their wives, which is perhaps why one must end up writing for them. Well, even the good literary magazines . . . not very many people *see* them . . .

True.

For better or worse. And, even when they do, it's often a year at *best,* after you've written the piece, before it comes out. In fact, you're probably lucky, if what you write one October is out in a magazine, available to even a small audience, by the next October.

Yes.

So, in a sense, you're *always* writing for the future. It's just that, when you *do* get older, the . . . future seems nearer. (Laughter.) So, ideally, I would like to write for an audience who knows the same things I do, and in fact, who have shared the same experiences I've had. (Laughter.) That's impossible; you can't multiply yourself . . .

But there is a way, I think . . . when I think, now, of the audience for poetry—no matter how many of those people may be, actually, poets . . . I mean I do have the sense that they, the people, say, at poetry readings, I do share something with them.

Well, it's *mostly* other poets who can read what you write, though, don't you think? I don't mind that. I think poets are human beings, too, and part of the citizenry, and deserving to be, and so I don't mind thinking it's mostly poets who read what I write. Well, that's *fine*. It's better, surely, because they know a bit more about what I'm actually doing. Musicians like to please other musicians. Politicians admire other politicians professionally. (Laughter.) Of course, the politician has to appeal to the people in other ways, but . . . You see what I mean, though. I don't see the fact that the biggest audience for poetry is other poets can be held against poetry in any way, or against the poet. And at readings, I feel that I am one of the best people a poet can possibly read to, because I have a chance of knowing what is going on. I myself prefer to read to audiences which number quite a few professionals, or would-be professionals. . . . I like that best.

I would agree with that. Do you think the audience for poetry at readings, and also those who buy books of poetry, has changed much in the past few years?

How many are a few years?

I guess I mean the last twelve or fifteen years. I remember, for example, at the height of the Vietnam . . . resistance—people would participate in poetry, go to poetry readings, although they sometimes did so out of political reasons.

Yes . . .

And so there was a peculiar, although healthy, kind of patronization of poetry.

Yes, there is no uniting cause at the moment; there are one or two, perhaps, in the offing, which would . . .

The nuclear . . .

Yes, gatherings in which people would share such public feelings and allow poetry to be a part of it. That was an interesting historical moment, and different from what went before it. I was thinking the other day that when I was in college, in the 1940s, the only poet I ever heard give a reading was Robert Frost, and very few other poets ever did or were asked to. I think maybe . . . John Gould Fletcher gave a reading or a lecture at the college I was then going to, but I didn't go. I knew his work. (Laughter.) Though now I *would* go, if he were still alive. I'd go, partly out of curiosity. But it just wasn't done—readings I mean. They were not cultural, or social, or artistic events. Something did happen to change that. I think Dylan Thomas' readings had a lot to do with the changes, and then there was the Vietnam *resistance* you mentioned. That's a good term for it. That had something to do with changing things for a while. Now, what have we got? A kind of vaudeville, I think.

You mean in poetry readings?

Yes. By and large the poets who are most appreciated by good-sized audiences are those who can entertain best, in between the poems, as it were. I don't at all mind that as a sociological development, but it has little or no bearing on whether the poetry matters or not. Still, it has become a crucial part of most poetry readings.

There's another thing: almost everybody who does many readings must have developed two or three poems which even if they may not have been written with this in mind, can be recognized as pretty well designed to get a response at poetry readings, and if your reading isn't going too well, you can always stick one of those in and pick up the tempo.

There's nothing wrong with that if you regard the reading itself as entertainment—show-biz rather than art. Which is the way I've begun to see it. In readings you get a certain public recognition, which really is your due if you're any good as a writer, and which you're not likely to get otherwise, and you get a little cash, too, not . . . usually enough, but some. Which is also your due if you're any good as a writer, and which you're also not likely to get any other way. So I think this society, with a curious perversity, has worked out a way of giving you what you merit, but for the wrong reasons.

Right. (Laughter.)

That's how I regard poetry readings. Actually, it's a kind of . . . what's the term for it? . . . a sort of guilt payment by universities for not doing better by literary culture.

Yes, could be. There is also, at times, an attempt by universities to acquire culture, I suppose, though this must be a part of a much larger desire in American culture.

I think it is. Yes, I think that's true. Of course, poets are a very small piece of the action.

I wanted to ask you one thing about working habits. Zbigniew Herbert once said that there were two kinds of poets on earth—the ox poet and the cat poet. The ox poet goes out every morning and works hard, from one end of the field to the other, and at the end of the day he has so much land that he's taken back from dissolution. The cat poet, on the other hand, doesn't do much of that at all, in fact he sleeps most of the day, and only hunts when he's hungry. But when he does hunt, he hunts very well. I was wondering where you might place yourself.

(Laughter.) Well, that's very funny. Which was Herbert? He was a cat poet?

He was a cat poet.

Yes, it sounds as though the person offering those descriptions favors the cats of the world. Which I would, too, I mean . . . if I had to be either an ox or a cat, in that sense, then I'm certainly a cat. But I'm the kind of cat who envies the ox.

I do, too, but why?

There was one period in my life when I was determined to write something every day, and I really enjoyed doing that. It lasted about two-and-a-half months, and I wrote some things that, at the time, I liked very much. And then I had to do a poetry reading, and did it, and read what I'd been writing, and somehow I couldn't get back . . . I'd stayed up too late that night, or something. I broke my habit pattern; I never have been able to get back into it, and I still look back on that period as being a sort of ten-weeks' Eden. And that's one of the reasons: because I had the experience of being an ox, very briefly. But . . . I can't do it.

Do a lot of things you wrote during those months . . . do they survive?

I wrote two parts of a long poem . . . and I think they're still good. I was going to put them into this book, *Selected Poems*. . . . Nobody else liked them, so I left them out. (Laughter.) I had decided that, if the friends I showed them to thought they really didn't stand up, I was outvoted.

Yes, well . . . could be. But how did you go about putting that book together?

Well, I read through everything that I had published, and those poems I'd always wanted to change I tried to change. I also knew in advance a number of poems that I was going to be very happy to leave out, without making any effort to change. So I went through my first book and left out everything I was certain should be left out and . . . those things I was in doubt about I tried to make better—testing them in that way, you know. And then went through the second book, and the third book, and all the poems since . . . and going back through old things, I began to find a few poems that had been lost, so to speak, or put aside, and I tried to rescue some of those. Those that I could read over and over again without feeling embarrassed about I put into the first version of the manuscript, and a few people saw it, Henri Coulette and Mark Strand and Harry Ford at Atheneum—and when things survived my looking them over, and their looking them over, and a few months of just sitting around, then I put everything that was left together, in a sort of chronological order. I went through everything I'd ever done of which I still had a copy.

One thing I wanted to ask you about, and that's the matter, the whole question of revision. To explain the question: when I began writing, it seemed much easier to write complete, whole poems at more or less one sitting. And over the years, it's become increasingly difficult to do that. I don't know. I think it has to do with the way the poems have changed, and have placed other, maybe more difficult demands on what I'm doing. But nevertheless, I think I find that I generally get a first draft, and then I work on it for about two weeks, rarely less. And of course sometimes I'll look at it, even months later, and say: Well, no, it's not right. Is revising something you think people learn how to do, or do certain poems close themselves off to you forever?

Both things are probably true, and there are probably three or four other things that are true as well. One of the reasons poems seem easier to write when you're starting out is that you don't know enough to see how hard they are, and you may find one way of doing things at the start that you can manage, and so you do it. You don't even realize that you could be doing it a little differently. But later the pressure of trying to do things differently enters into the composition, and especially into the revision. In one sense, then, the more you know the harder it is. On the other hand, I think there's a compensation: the more you know, the more chances you have of getting it right.

Yes.

And I think that matters—to try to get it right. I have not very often had the experience of getting a first draft right in one sitting. It must show in my writing, to some degree, anyhow. What happens to me in the first sitting is that I become able to think of *what is going to happen*. It's like a mental first draft, or a *spiritual* first draft. (Laughter.) But the links, the phrasings . . .

Oh, that's all I mean, only the broadest outline . . . sometimes only a wishful outline.

But I like getting as much as I can the first time. Then the revising is a lot easier. I went back to poems I had written, oh, twenty-five or more years ago and tried to improve them, and one of the things I found was that sometimes—I don't mean to dramatize this but sometimes the text as it already existed really did resist any sort of tampering. I would change a phrase, or change the rhythm, and for intelligent and sensitive reasons, and with a certain skill, and yet it wouldn't seem right. Now that was probably because I'd got used to the text as it had existed for years, but I think there was more to it than that, also. At least when that happened, when I'd given it my best try, I would give up tampering with it. Maybe I still didn't like what I'd originally said, but I could believe that the standing version had *some* validity because I could no longer budge it. And this happened more often than I would have expected it to.

I would imagine that it would, in your work.

Certainly in a way I was pleased to discover that. On the other hand, I must say I was still disappointed that I hadn't been able to . . . well, there was some idea of perfection that I had in mind which I wasn't able to live up to. For years I'd been looking forward to the moment when I could change something—this or that detail—and make it better, make it right. I was unable to do that, in many cases. Here and there I think I did come close, and that was enough, I suppose. I think most people who read the book will hardly notice the changes. But I did and do; and as I say, I write, first of all, for myself.

Sure, yes. One other question: the region you come from, Florida, and I guess the South generally, seem to occur in your work, or inhabit your work, but not necessarily with any regularity or consistency. For example, it seems to be a part of The Summer Anniversaries, *and then seems to some extent to move out of the way in* Night Light, *and then it comes back again, more localized and particularized, in, say, the Vallejo poem in* Departures, *and in the poem "Childhood."*

It's just the way things worked out, you know.

There's no sort of conscious push toward . . .

No. In the poems I have been thinking of and writing the last few years, I have grown aware that that was a subject somehow available to me all over again. The perspective of time and distance alters substance somewhat, and so it is possible to think freshly of things that were once familiar and ordinary as if they had become strange again. I don't know whether this is true of everybody's experience, but at a certain point childhood seems mythical once more. It did to start with, and it does suddenly again.

In that poem, "Childhood," you mention Crane, Alberti, Rimbaud, and Wordsworth—and all of them I can see sort of helping *in the poem. And that's been, in a way, my idea of what influences ought to be, and I can feel them helping you write that poem—which seems to be totally a Donald Justice poem by Donald Justice.*

OK, good.

I also like the marginalia.

Thanks. The desire to try the marginalia had been with me a long time. Crane in *The Bridge* is one of the models, and of course Coleridge, and there are others. The poem began out of Alberti, out of Alberti's poems from the 1920s. Then quite early it became . . . less indebted to Alberti. There are passages in Crane . . . passages in which suddenly he thinks of something that happened to him in his childhood that he, as it were, cannot *forgive*. Suddenly his mother smiles at him, and he simply cannot forgive her for having smiled only that once, if I remember it right. It's in *The Bridge* and something else is going on, but suddenly his childhood is illuminated, even though it's not at the moment his main subject . . . and of course Rimbaud is marvelous about his childhood, in "Les Poètes de sept ans" most particularly, as far as I'm concerned. And in *The Prelude*, Wordsworth has those wonderful recollections of transformation and transcendence coming from what would seem like ordinary, or almost ordinary, experiences of childhood and adolescence, in which he is moved, and the world is moved with him. Alberti is less well known in this country, despite Mark Strand's efforts, and yet some of the poems of the 1920s and on into the 1930s in which he remembers his childhood seem to me to be marvelous in much the same way. It is as if a new, visionary, Wordsworthian gleam falls upon the ordinary, and transforms it. And I would like to have illuminated the fragmented recollections of my own childhood in a similar way—at least that was the impulse, the desire. For the time being, I think of it as my favorite among my own poems. I know only three or four other people who can still remember the Miami of the thirties as it comes through in that poem—but I would like to think that it is there, in the poem, to be remembered by anybody who would like to keep it, if only—and unavoidably—secondhand.

(1979)

An Interview with David Hamilton and Lowell Edwin Folsom

Let's begin by asking about Selected Poems *because that, after all, is the occasion for this interview. We'd like you to tell us something of how it came together out of your other collections. In the notes at the back you describe its arrangement as a "fair chronological order." That's a curious qualification.*

I didn't realize that would be ambiguous. I meant "approximate." After so long it's difficult to know exactly when you wrote something. I didn't want to say the poems were arranged in chronological order because I couldn't be quite sure of that. But as well as I could reconstruct the history of it these are in order. In some cases I'm positive of the sequence because it meant something to me at the time.

Do you keep notebooks and dated papers?

I do now but I didn't in the past. I've become more compulsive instead of less. In quite a few cases I can remember where or when I wrote a certain poem. One poem I remember writing on Memorial Day, 1954. We were supposed to go to a couple of parties and I kept saying, "Let's wait until I finish this, it won't be long now." It took me all day and well into the night, so we didn't make the parties.

You can probably remember when you wrote a poem more easily than many other things.

Perhaps. But I do generally remember where and when I saw movies, for instance, and I can remember where I read most novels. I read *Madame Bovary* in the railroad station in Portland, Maine.

Sometimes you have remembered very precisely, as with, for example, the poem "Fragment: To a Mirror," which has two dates, 1963–1972. Was that one you returned to and finished?

Yes, I had started it in 1963. I keep notes while working on poems—phrases, lines, passages, perhaps only words—if anything at all seems promising in the project. I had gone back to the notes for this one more than once to try to make something out of them. And finally, when preparing *Departures*, I just decided I would do what I could with those old notes, and if I couldn't do anything I'd throw them away. They'd been around long enough. I left out a great deal of the ambitious scaffolding for the poem but did get it whittled down to what I could accept.

When you say you keep notes . . .

I mean all the paper that has been written or scribbled on while working out the poem.

I had a remarkable experience once. I was working on a poem that wasn't going anywhere, but once in a while you can rescue something from the wreckage of the notes. I'd been fiddling with this particular poem off and on for two or three years, and one night I made a little progress. So when I was free to work on it again, three or four nights later, I looked around for the notes containing those small advances. I couldn't find them. I'd spent thirty minutes looking for them, I guess, when I gave up and decided to start back at the point I'd started before. I worked perhaps till midnight and again made a little progress. Well, the next time I came to work on the poem, I found both sets of notes and they were almost identical, almost word for word, including scratchings out. Oh, I thought, I'm really doing marvelously well on this poem; I must have found what has to be done. I have a sort of Platonic notion that somewhere ideally exists the poem I'm trying to write, if only I can find it, and here I had this excellent testimony, a sign that I was on the right track. As it happens, I finished the poem and it wasn't very good. I published it, but it's not in *Selected Poems*. I had been mistaken, you know; the signs were wrong. Very disappointing, considering all the work I put into it, and the signs.

I picture lots of papers around, in cardboard boxes and desk drawers.

Boxes, and now I have a fine filing cabinet that I've been picking through in preparation for going away for the year. Yes, it has a lot of stuff in it. And I've thrown things away as well.

One of the things you have to do now is decide which poems to take along.

Yes, that's right, and that was interesting. I'm taking five poems and four plays. Plays are what I want to try to work on this year, but I have a few poems too that I haven't quite finished.

Are any of these poems of Tremayne? We've seen three of those, two in Selected Poems *and another in the* New Yorker. *They suggest a series.*

That most recent Tremayne poem is one that was left over from *Selected Poems;* I hadn't been able to finish it. There was meant to be a group of four poems, and two of them simply weren't finished in time for the book. In a fourth Tremayne poem, still not done, I have, maybe, twenty versions of the last stanza, and I'm not satisfied. I'd like to get it out of the way. I've spent more than enough time on it already and probably should settle for one of the versions I have, but I know there is something better. What I seem to have been doing this year is simply trying to finish whatever I could not finish before.

Actually that seems to be the condition I'm often in, and not just after a book. There always seem to be notes and bits of things and fragments lying around and I keep trying to complete them, put them together. It's a little bit like—I don't know whether you have this compulsion or not—trying to make the meat and the bread come out together. If you don't, you have to take a little bit more of one or the other. Well, there always seem to be notes spilling over from poems just finished. An endless process, thank goodness.

When did you know the Tremayne poems were going to be a series of four?

Early. Four happens to be one of those literary numbers, like three or nine. I noticed that in the first couple of Tremaynes seasons were mentioned. And I thought, Aha, one for each season. Someone with the sense of design I have is always looking for ways to make things go together, and a set of seasons adding up to four would make the kind of obvious sense that appeals to me. It turned out that the third one didn't have anything to do with a season; nevertheless that was part of the idea.

It spoke of seasons of the day: "And something starts all over, call it day."

Right but . . . the last one, what I think will be the last one—I don't know, if I enjoy doing them and have another workable idea I wouldn't necessarily keep to my own limit—but the fourth and last one I intend to write is about autumn.

We were wondering about changes in Selected Poems. *One revision I wanted to ask you about was "Sonatina in Yellow," a poem I'm very fond of.*

What did I change, the end?

Right. Originally it was, "Repeat it now, no one was listening. / Repeat it, the air, the variations."

Ah, yes.

Why did you remove the line, "Repeat it, the air, the variations"?

Well, I always had had trouble with what I think of as the coda of this poem, the last little paragraph. Now what it should do, I felt from the start, was repeat or take up again motifs, or motives even, to speak of the question musically, from what had gone before. Now the "air" is a pun on the dead air of summer mentioned earlier in the poem and also on a musical air. That much is obvious. The "variations" would have to do with musical form as well—also of course with the verbal variations on the phrases and as a consequence on the themes that appear earlier in the poem. In that sense it fitted in the coda, but it seemed to me that it slowed things down a good deal. It was in there merely for a sort of formal reason. It was doing its *job*. And I wanted whatever I had in there at the end to be doing more than its job. I'm glad you like the poem, because I like it too, but I'm worried about some of its features. Particularly there at the end. When I first sent in the text for the book, the "Repeat it now" line was also gone. Finally I thought I needed one "repeat" line but not two. Who knows? Listen, the first time I finished this poem, there were crows flying around through several of the stanzas.

And you got all the crows out.

And kept them out.

It seems like a willful thing to do, putting crows in a sonatina in yellow.

Well, the poem is in a way about death, and they seemed to me, with their blackness, to associate very well with that. Also their harsh music. But they were too symbolical really.

One of the things I was wondering about taking south with me was the notes on this poem. I haven't given up on this. It has a prose commentary intended to accompany the verse text which I haven't shown to anybody. Still, I decided finally to leave all this behind in the filing cabinet. I didn't want to get hung up on that again. I've spent a lot of time on this poem and on the other sonatina and on a couple of other sonatinas I haven't published. But one day I may get it right, in which case it will have a prose commentary, and that prose commentary will describe a descent into the underworld, a legendary sort of descent. Because that is implied in this poem. The prose commentary will bring out undertones and make them much stronger perhaps. All speculative, of course.

So when you come to offering a prose commentary as in "Childhood," the last poem in the volume, that's not something that you've just happened upon.

It's an idea I've wanted to put to work for a long time. Once the notion of a prose commentary enters your head, it's hard to get out. You'd like not only to write the poems but to write the commentary, you know; don't leave that up to the others, who're likely to get it wrong anyhow.

Do you have models in mind for that kind of writing?

Coleridge, Hart Crane. But I wasn't able to do it as they did it. I wanted to write elevated, mystical, highly charged prose. I just couldn't screw my courage up to that—or my style, more likely.

Prose that would be more rhetorical than the poetry?

Yes, exactly.

And that would serve as some sort of ironic counterpoint to the poetry?

Yes, in the commentaries on the sonatinas which I have, but which I haven't been able to get right, that is indeed the case. I was reading some of *The Bridge* marginalia yesterday and it's a prose much more as I would want it, you know, nicely florid and elevated.

And yet I have to acknowledge that one of the afflictions of American verse at present is the prose poem, and one reason it is an affliction instead of a salvation is that poets allow themselves all sorts of licenses regarding rhetoric, elevation, diction, and foolish ideas that they wouldn't think of allowing themselves in their so-called verse. I've been saying to my students in the last few years, "Your prose has got to be at least as well-written as your poetry," because most of them really do write their poems more conscientiously than they do their prose. Maybe we've come to another historical moment.

You've expressed a conviction that there really is no such thing as organic meters, that you can't imitate the sea, breathing, the heartbeat.

I do think that. I may be wrong, but that is a conviction.

You also believe that music is the one art that does not have as its motive memory.

So far as I can experience the arts that is true.

Given these two convictions, I'm surprised that I find music entering your poetry at the moments of most intense memory.

I knew you were working up to some sort of paradox.

In "Memory of a Porch," "I heard / The thing begin— / A thin, skeletal music," or in "Absences," "Like the memory of scales descending the white keys." The sonatinas themselves, especially the "Sonatina in Yellow," are intense poems of memory, I think, and your sonatina form apparently tries to imitate music in language.

I think I can account superficially for what you're pointing out, which I hadn't noticed before. I think it may be because my own memory happens to be rich in memories of music. I have felt very strongly about music at times. So recollections of music come back to me naturally enough sometimes when emotion approaches. I mean quite naturally out of experience, rather than from any theory involving hierarchies or distinctions among the arts.

What about the sonatina form then?

The sonatina form is really very simple. I'd wanted to try a quasi-musical form and the simplest of all among the classical possibilities, it seemed, would be the precursor of the sonata form, the sonatina, in which you only really had to have two parts, two themes. I didn't want to get into a complicated sonata-allegro, even if it could be done. I certainly didn't want to get into any sort of complicated set of quasi-musical forms such as you find in the "Four Quartets," or *think* you have found after reading the criticism. It seemed to me that you might wish to start modestly. The sonatina is a modest classical form which involves an A part and a B part. It involves saying A again and saying B again in a key different from the one it was said in the first time around.

The only thing I had to find was an A thing to say and a B thing to say, and—which was trickier—a way to change the key of B. The form also allows a little freedom; you can either say A B A B or you can say A B B A or you can say A plus transition plus B, you know, or you can put a coda or several codas at the end. There's a little flexibility, a little give. I tried to find a change of key, a modulation, which would be linguistic or grammatical rather than musical. So I worked all these schemes out in advance of writing the poem; that was part of the pleasure of the whole business for me at the time. And it seemed to me that one of the ways of modulating, grammatically, would be to change the *tense;* another might be to change the *person.* I've forgotten now, but I worked out four or five of these; I guess one was to change from interrogation to declaration. But then I felt it really wasn't literarily interesting just to repeat A if there were more than two or three lines to it; so I modified A, which also happens in the musical form, at least as it moves toward the sonata-allegro form—you get into development sections.

To think about something else allowed me to write about what I was interested in, but indirectly, from an angle. I hadn't meant when I started "Sonatina in Yellow" to write about my father. But I did have as a general idea in all the sonatinas the mythic or legendary theme of descending into the underworld, and once I began mentally or spiritually or esthetically to descend into the underworld I found my father.

Had he been dead then for some time?

For thirteen years. But I hadn't written any poems about him. So I need not have been surprised to find him there.

Are musical forms generally available to you?

Not so much what I would call forms—but yes, vaguely musical possibilities, though I think "musical" as a critical term referring to effects of sound in poetry is much overused, abused even. I am interested in the musical sounding of the words in some poems, and in a few places I have gone to some trouble to make these sounds linguistically rich; but I haven't loaded up the sonatinas in this way. They're probably a little more musical in this primitive fashion, that is, in the mere sounding of their words, than most of what I would write, but it's the *structure* of the music that I was interested in imitating, not otherwise the sound. I would be interested in trying to write something in another musical form sometime. I've tried the blues but that's even simpler.

You did that in the "Uncollected" section of Selected Poems.

I was using up what I knew about the blues in the two I included in the book and in four or five others I wrote at the same time but didn't publish. I may publish three or four more some time, but . . .

So you have more blues songs around.

Oh yes, but by now I've almost forgotten which lines come from traditional blues and which ones I've invented. I know they don't sound like Mississippi Delta blues, for instance, but then I didn't want them to, I'm not from the Mississippi Delta. I wanted them to be a sort of "literary blues." As Coleridge's "Rime" is a "literary ballad," say.

The blues lend themselves more to poetry because they have words built into them.

Yes, that's quite right.

And the sonatina is a much more abstract form.

Absolutely, but I do believe poetry is capable of being structured in terms that can be described abstractly. There may be half a dozen schools of theory which can't entertain that notion, but not to do so is an historical and esthetic blindness both. Obviously there is room for abstract structure in any esthetic design. There may be no necessity for it, but there is room for it.

But in the case of the sonatina you had some sense of that abstract structure when you began, while in other cases you may discover the structure along the way.

Actually I discovered the sonatina along the way too because although I knew what a *musical* sonatina was and I'd played many sonatinas on the piano, I didn't know what a sonatina in poetry would be until I had tried to write one. I don't think it turned out to be what I might ideally have imagined a literary sonatina to be, but it's similar. It's as close as I've been able to get, and I think it's as close as anybody's been able to get to a musical form in poetry—musical *form*, that is, so far as the structural outline goes.

The synesthesia in the titles mixes an aural form with a visual image; why did you add color to the musical structure?

Several reasons, but one was simply to emphasize the abstraction because the colors, musically speaking, must seem abstract. Actually in the text of the poems, there's very little reference to the color; it's background. There would be more reference to color in the prose commentary, but at least once in each of the poems, I think maybe only once, there's a reference to it. Yellow seemed to me eventually to associate with decay. And green with freshness. Not very original associations. The simple practical reason for the titles, however, was that I had bought in the university bookstore a four-color notebook to start writing the poems in, and one of the four colors was green and one was yellow, one was blue and one was pink. Pink was very hard; blue I almost managed, but not pink.

Is a "Sonatina in Blue" one of the sets of notes you're taking along?

No, I decided not to take it, I've given up on blue.

Are those five poems you're taking along new or old poems?

One goes back to the fall of 1974, the one I'm most serious about, but it's very hard and may end up rather long. It's in several parts and I've finished maybe two parts of it, or three. I don't know what will eventually become of it, but I must finish it. And the Tremayne poem I'm still working at I started in the fall of 1977. That happened to have a date on it in my notes. All of these are failures, you might say, up to this point. They're poems I haven't been able to get right but that I have had some hopes for. The same with the plays. One of the plays I started in 1964 and I think the beginning of it is really very good, but it's hard to go on with.

Will the plays be easier to complete than the poems?

No, I don't think so. I know more about writing poems than I do about writing plays, so the poems really are easier.

Can you tell us something about the plays?

I don't think I should spoil them by talking too much about them. But I can say that one of them has to do with Lorca. One of the things I've done so far is to translate some Lorca poems not just into American but into what I think of as a sort of California language of the future. Not of the distant future, but if something like the death of Lorca were to occur in America, California would be the most likely place, wouldn't it? But that's enough on that, I think.

Another play you've been working on is an updating of The Tempest, *isn't it?*

Yes, right.

Is part of your updating that it's no longer verse drama at all?

What I've written of it is definitely not verse, it's prose. The updating amounted to a complete rethinking. *The Tempest* was going to be a kind of ideal model in the back of my mind which perhaps no one would ever think of in seeing the play. In the first version—it has now been changed a little—Caliban was going to be the second son of the Prospero character, and was going to be an auto mechanic by occupation and an amateur of the viola da gamba. It really should be Ariel, I guess, who plays this instrument, but I thought Caliban, who speaks so beautifully in the play—"The isle is full of noises"—ought to have it. Well, you know, I was just amusing myself by making false analogies.

Deflected analogies.

Yes, yes, that's better.

You do that all the time.

Well, yes, perhaps so. I don't know whether I'll be able to write these two plays or not but I'm going to try.

You mentioned four plays.

The other two are short, and whether anything will come of them or not I don't know. One is called "Faust: A Skit"—a farce, partly in verse. The other is called "The Whistler" and is about anti-Semitism.

These are subjects you would not feel like dealing with in poems?

I suppose not. Anti-Semitism, for instance. I don't know quite why, but early in life I was probably too much influenced by Poe's theory of poetry. Poems were not to be didactic, for example. I no longer think that's true, but I must have been affected by it.

I think poetry ought to be capable of dealing with any-thing. I mean, I do basically believe that. On the other hand, for me, it's very difficult to write a poem about something I could write an essay on.

Maybe it's because in something like anti-Semitism there aren't many permissible views.

Well, the forbidden view has lately begun to become more and more permissible, apparently. Your point is a good one, but I think the unthinkable is becoming acceptable again, and I find that tragic, after the experience of the thirties and forties. This week I've been reading newspapers from the thirties because my wife happened to buy some from an an-tique dealer a few years ago. They're fascinating. One of the stories that keep cropping up, on the front page of course, concerns whatever the latest decree of the Nazi government may have been. These decrees are treated just like ordinary news stories. And I remember how horrible it became. The theme comes around again these days; it begins to matter a lot. Even so, I can't see myself writing a poem directly about it.

Can we return once more to "Sonatina in Yellow"?

Yes.

The epigraph is from Rilke, "Your quickly vanishing photograph in my more slowly vanishing hand." That strikes me as applicable to all your work.

I think it might be.

It's applicable for a number of reasons, not the least of which is the reference to photographs. You've talked about poems at their best transmuting subjective experience into an object, and have said that that object at its best would be like a snapshot. It would be a memory captured that you could come back to and deal with because it's there now in an object.

I do believe that, yes.

The experience of many of your poems, for me, is the experience of reading a sensitive description of a snapshot or photograph, a photo that you care for greatly. I wonder how many of your poems actually are based on snapshots?

I don't think any of them are except the one I just finished, and even that wasn't a snapshot; it was a photograph by Walker Evans, a scene in Alabama in the thirties. I do carry around a packet of photographs of my parents and of houses we used to live in and that sort of thing. I've never been able to use them. You might say they have become for me a sort of talisman. I keep thinking they will fructify. But I don't think any poems I've written, except this new one, are based on photographs. What they are based on, some of them, is memories of the way something looked at a certain time.

It's as if you were doing a photograph mentally, taking your own snapshot.

Yes, that's right.

So making the poem, then, is more like making a photograph than like describing one?

That's right.

In "Memories of the Depression Years" there are three memories, at three-year intervals, and those are the snapshotlike moments that stand out?

Yes, that's right.

Are there more that you're working on?

I certainly meant to write an endless series, but those were the only three I've managed to finish. I have no other notes on hand. I do mean to remain alert to the possibility of doing others that would fit into such a series, but I haven't got any.

Now that you've written a poem describing the Walker Evans photograph, what's the difference between writing that poem and creating the "photograph" or "snapshot" out of your memory?

I felt more limited in this case. I didn't want to depart from the facts of the photograph, which anybody else could look at too, and check up on. So I think the poem will seem esthetically cooler. I like to think that many of my poems seem objective and well-distanced, but I think this poem may be even more so. I was interested in it as practice, and indeed I've tried to write others; but I haven't been able to, and I've just about given up on the idea. I wanted to see what the answer would be to the question you just put to me, I think. I did not put as much of myself into it, and my own experience, though the scene was the kind of scene I recall from childhood.

I was going to ask what attracted you to the photograph. It was not a purely esthetic attraction?

No, it wasn't; it made a connection with my own life and the life of my relatives in the South in the thirties. I would like to be able to say, and it would be partly true, that it was like a photograph made of a long-ago part of my life.

This was a farm family?

No, it's a photograph sometimes identified as "Mule Team and Poster." It depicts a brick wall of what appears to be a warehouse. It's in Alabama in 1936, but I don't think it's in *Let Us Now Praise Famous Men*. It's just one of the Farm Security Administration photographs; it depicts a brick wall of what appears to be a warehouse in front of which a couple of mules are standing, munching corn shucks on the arid-looking earth, and there's a poster of a Silas Green traveling show peeling from the wall. It's really quite beautiful, and I'm sure that one of my interests in it, one of the secrets of its appeal to me, was that the manifest content of the photograph was ugly and unpleasant—and I myself knew that ugliness and un-pleasantness because I had been in Alabama in 1936, and in the summertime, and it really was like a photograph of some-thing I could almost remember. My father was from Ala-bama, farther south than where this photograph was made, and we used to visit our relatives over there, poor farmers and store clerks and so on. There seemed to be a lot of this sort of thing—brick walls and mules standing in front of them, and posters advertising movies or traveling shows. Out of this very unattractive but quite sympathetic scene, an ar-rangement of great beauty, I thought, had come forth, through Evans. Art! Art having occurred, I wanted to try to multiply that art. And then last week I spent trying to de-scribe another Evans photograph and wasn't able to.

What do you mean? That you found that what you thought to say about it just doesn't interest you once it's said?

In part. I simply was not able to see enough in the photograph to make saying so much worthwhile. The words were not paying off with a high enough quotient of what Aristotle would have called "thought"—what I call "perception." So it just wasn't worth it. I could describe the thing perfectly well, in a somewhat heavy style, as luck would have it, but once I'd done that, it didn't make any difference. It didn't make enough difference. With the first of Evans' photographs I judged that I had seen enough in it to make the saying count.

Had your father grown up on a farm in Alabama?

Yes, he had been born in southern Alabama and then as a youth he moved over to a part of Georgia adjoining Alabama which looked just like it as far as I could tell. This was a part of my summers growing up, not a part I really liked.

Are you aware much of generations beyond, say, your grandfather?

Not much beyond great-grandfathers, no. I can't account for it, perhaps because we were always poor, but on neither side of my family do recollections go back beyond what would be my great-grandparents—except for a story about a woman ancestor on my father's side who became a stowaway to North Carolina supposedly because she had committed some technical offense against a king or a king's property, a king's forest perhaps. Maybe she poached. But such stories grow to be a little like myths; you don't know how much to credit them. And there aren't many such stories in my family, unhappily. I wish there were.

Have you always been fascinated with family albums and looking at pictures?

I didn't know that I was, but I was; my mother was, and she thrust them upon me from the start.

When you were working on the Evans photograph, did you think of Williams' Pictures from Brueghel?

Absolutely. It would be awfully hard not to. I once tried writing a series of poems on Hopper paintings and they sounded like Williams' Brueghel poems, but defective somehow. Yes, the Williams poems are very powerful; it would be hard to resist them. But I tried to, not quite successfully.

When I was young, I was interested in writing very elaborate syntax. Some of the poets I liked a lot were interesting in part because of their syntax. Yeats sometimes has a very elaborate syntax. And I wanted to try that. Even Williams, though he looks simple, has a very elaborate syntax, and this challenged me. But then at some point comes the desire to purify, to simplify, and that has, you know, begun to appeal to me more and more.

One of the things that interest me syntactically now is the use of fragments, as in the last line of "Thinking about the Past," which goes "Dusks, dawns; waves; the ends of songs . . ." I don't know that anybody else likes or ought to like that, but I like the line myself and in part because it's just like little bits of consciousness floating up. Touches of a brush, say. It seems to me that fragments sometimes can have that effect. The first time I recall really liking fragments myself and seeing powerful possibilities in them was in reading Alberti, who uses sentence fragments beautifully, dramatically. Ever since, I've tried to do something with them. Of course I don't at all mean the notational style you see frequently, ever since the Imagists at least, and not only in amateur verses—as if to suppress a verb were to write a line.

Whether we're talking about elaborate or simplified syntax, or about fragments for that matter, we're talking about kinds of technical proficiency.

Yes, there are properties which I think belong unarguably to poetry, and one of them is *technical virtue*. I don't know how else to put that, but without it poetry dies. I think, on the other hand, poetry can live on the strength of technical virtue alone, but it only lives a sort of half-life then. When you write, you have to be willing to settle for that, I think, but what you really desire is something whole; large, even. Poetry at its best is fulfilling its nature most entirely when it has a great mastery of form, or technique, and shows considerable, though perhaps a hidden or disguised, interest in its own formal or technical character. Otherwise it might as well be prose. I love prose, and it really *might* as well be prose. Now once poetry has this, it is of course much better if what is said proves interesting and intelligent and intelligible and true and perceptive and has all those virtues one would expect even of expository prose. And of course it becomes even better if the themes it deals with are grand. A seven-line poem ought to be better than a six-line poem, all other things being equal, simply because it contains more. But all those things are not equal, and what is basic and absolutely necessary is formal and technical character; otherwise the poem will be forgotten eventually, or remembered only for something like the personality or history of the poet, or the fact that he may have been the first or the loudest to deal with a certain topic, or something of that sort. Well, that is of a certain interest, too. I don't wish to deny it. But for the art of poetry itself, basic is some formal or technical interest. That does not mean that anyone can or should prescribe the nature of that formal or technical interest in advance of the occasion. That always remains to be defined, or ought always to remain to be defined, for the various occasions, and by the age. But I think it is absolutely essential.

Many poets today would say that memory seeks out its own meter, but in a very real way, with you, meter seeks out memory, right?

Well, I'm willing to go with that version, though it seems an extreme way of putting it.

It's an extreme reversal, but you've talked about meter as a kind of substantiation of your poetry, even as a "fixative" of memory.

If you're working in meter in the first place—you don't have to work in meters, in the kind of meters I'm thinking of—but if you are, then to get it wrong proves to you that you haven't even, as I would suggest, *remembered* right. If you commit yourself, if you give yourself over to the meters, they have to be right. If you don't, well, that's a different story.

If we think less of meters than of form, much the same thing applies. In "Sonatina in Yellow," you hadn't been seeking out a way to talk about your father in a particular form, but the form you devised gave you the memory of your father.

In a sense that's true, yes. It is a false notion, I am sure, to propose that poetry comes only from subject, is never more than an extension of content, as has all too often been rather pompously said. Poetry comes from anywhere, and the subject is certainly a major source, probably the major source. If you have something you care a lot about, then you may well write a poem about it, may indeed be driven to do so. But it can come from elsewhere—just as a composition in music may come from merely fooling around. Or from thinking: This time I'll try D minor; or, I like what Handel wrote just there, I think I'll try some variations on it. It comes from anywhere, and as far as I'm concerned, there should be no hierarchy of values in the consideration of this. What matters is the result, not the source, the origin, or the theory.

Your history so far seems to suggest a particular interest in seeking conscious deflections from established forms. I'd see that interest in deflection as central, as you say, to the "formal or technical character" of your work.

I would be willing to think so.

In "Variations for Two Pianos," for example, were you thinking of the villanelle when you started the poem?

Of course.

And simultaneously thinking of not *doing the villanelle.*

Yes, exactly. The villanelle is practically impossible, at least in English, and I don't know of any villanelle in our language that doesn't have at least one waste stanza in it. There seems to me no obligation to carry on with a proper villanelle when it may mean including one or two stanzas less good than the others. So you may end up with a pseudo-villanelle if you're going to do one, unless you happen to be very lucky and get the whole thing. A double villanelle, even. I can imagine that, but it would be hard to find.

What do you mean by "get" and "find"?

"Find" may be the better word for it. I mean something like going on a voyage of discovery in the old days, or prospecting, digging for precious metals.

The sestinas are another example; they avoid the usual sestina metrics.

When I was writing those sestinas, I think practically all the sestinas that had been written in English before, the ones I had read anyway, were in iambic pentameter—or at least in what I would call a casual pentameter, one in which the line might get a little longer or a little shorter, as in Pound's or the two by Kees. But I consciously shortened the lines; I varied the length of the lines. Nowadays anybody may do that. The Katmandu sestina has a small place in the history of the form, I think.

In addition to specific deflected forms, groups of your poems sometimes deny expectations of patterns. In the gathering of three odes, for example, the "Cool Dark Ode" addresses night and suggests winter night; the "Warm Flesh-Colored Ode" suggests late summer. But what does the "Pale Tepid Ode" suggest? You set up a pattern, then jump track.

Well, on the other hand, it keeps to the track because you have "Cool Dark," "Warm Flesh-Colored" and what's left? Not much.

You reverse the placement of the adjectives—"Pale Tepid" rather than "Tepid Pale."

But that's the way it would be in speech probably; you wouldn't say "tepid pale." If you did, it would be like the overcareful Joycean placement of adjectives before a noun. It's just something other than the two that come before it—what's left? That's the way I thought of it. Sort of the bleaching out of colors, of definition. I don't know how to put it, but it seemed to me altogether obvious that "Pale Tepid" followed from "Cool Dark" and "Warm Flesh-Colored." Just set yourself that problem. What pair of adjectives having to do with color and temperature could possibly come next?

Well, given cool and warm, you'd have to say something like . . .

Lukewarm anyway, or pale, or tepid, or . . .

Terribly hot.

Sure, but that's not my style.

I'm fascinated that you say it seemed perfectly natural that that would be the completion. I think it's not perfectly natural to most people.

All right, OK, but I'm asking, well, "terribly hot," yes, all right. But what *color?* After dark and flesh-colored. If you had to have a third.

Well, "flesh-colored" seems mild. I might think of something harsh, say, "dazzling."

"Dazzling" might be good. I may write a fourth, "Hot Dazzling Ode."

If you do, you owe that one to us.

I do indeed. But look, one reason I like series and groups is because once you have a couple of poems connecting somewhere or associating in some way, another may be produced simply by thinking: What would be related, what would come out of, or what would connect with that? Anybody becomes inventive thinking along those lines.

I'm thinking of a pattern suggested by "Unflushed Urinals" and "Sunday Afternoon in Buffalo, Texas."

I consider the Walker Evans poem I spoke of as a third along those lines. They're American scenes, and I really feel I should take a couple more bus trips and see what turns up.

It has to be by bus?

Well, it seems so. The bus still shows you the America of the past. Plane rides, in this respect, don't seem to turn up anything. One of the great experiences of my married life was to take the bus from Albemarle, North Carolina to Palo Alto, California years ago. It was an awful and wonderful experience. Four nights and three days, or three nights and four days; I've forgotten which. And we'll never forget that trip.

Speaking of things American, do you see an American tradition that has influenced your own work, an American tradition in poetry that you look back toward?

I can say whom and what I like, that's about all. In America there is not just one line of evolution, one stream, despite the propaganda. As for American poets of the nineteenth century, I like Emerson; I think he's a good poet, and I like some of Melville's poems. I like Emily Dickinson very much; I think she's a very great poet. I like Trumbull Stickney; Tuckerman. And I respect Whitman, without having the kind of affection for him many people seem to have. The twentieth century begins for me with Edwin Arlington Robinson. And in this century the best poets seem so different from one another that any attempt to define an American tradition ought to involve some strong sense of the variety and the diversity and the going off in all directions. Emerson does not necessarily end up in James Dickey.

Hart Crane?

Hart Crane is a master, yes, in a few lines anyway. Such beauty as I hope not to be forgotten.

Ezra Pound?

Early Pound anyway, yes, a master. Thereafter, I don't know. Thereafter I think he became victimized by ideas. When that happens with poetry, something goes wrong, I believe, and I believe that happened to Pound. I know that not everyone thinks so, in fact most people probably don't. But just reading him for pleasure and his power of invention or recovery, for the beauty of sound and the shapeliness of his expression, the early poems seem certainly very fine—*Personae,* including of course *Cathay.*

Which of the American poets do you find yourself returning to and reading most?

Williams would be among them, certainly. Williams is so inventive, and he *does* hold up. Stevens of course is another. Eliot remains for me a great model of seriousness. His ideas are another matter, but . . . Well, let's see, Robinson I read frequently with pleasure, and Emily Dickinson. I shouldn't forget Frost, for years my favorite. Those are, I think, the main ones.

Do you subscribe to the separation of the Dickinson and Whitman traditions?

If it's forced upon me, I do. If there were an election in November, I'd go with Dickinson, the one with the more modest scope.

I sometimes hear Dickinson off-rhymes in your poetry.

Maybe so; I think off-rhymes can be very nice, but they may have come as much from incapacity as from remembering Dickinson.

Ransom, Tate, Warren?

Yes, I haven't gone back and read them lately, but they certainly were a formative influence. I wrote my master's thesis on them, and in a way I've always known their work. Ransom is a favorite.

You mentioned once that the first poet of note that you heard read was Robert Frost.

I don't think other poets were reading much in public then. I lived and went to school in Miami, where he wintered in the early forties, and he would read at the university. He would say at the end of the reading, "Now what are your favorites, what would you like to hear?" That used to embarrass me. I was studying composition with a composer named Carl Ruggles. At one of those readings, maybe the very first one I went to, Ruggles—who also came down from New England to winter there and who knew Frost—called up to the stage one of his favorites and I felt terribly embarrassed for those two great men. It seemed to me, in my juvenile way, not sophisticated. Come to think of it, it still does.

What about the European poets? Obviously the French and Spanish poets.

Mainly them; I don't really read any foreign language with great ease, and certainly I don't speak any. Those are the two that I know best. I worked hard to get acquainted with some poetry in German, postwar poetry, but French and Spanish I feel a little more comfortable with.

Is Alberti the master in that group for you?

Absolutely.

South American poets?

Oh yes, well, my favorite American poet in Spanish is a Mexican poet, Ramon López Velarde.

I don't know of him at all.

Paz calls him the father of Mexican poetry. He died about the time the First World War ended, at an early age, but I think he's a very great poet. H. R. Hays translated some of his poems during the Second World War, and he's been intermittently translated since, but there's never been a collection of translations and there should be; he's very good.

Let's go back to the Anglo-American poets briefly. When you go back to Williams, which periods or volumes do you favor?

Well, there are two moments in his career that I particularly like. One is the *Spring and All* period, 1922 or thereabouts. The other is the *Pictures from Brueghel* period, postwar, indeed post-*Paterson*. For me those are the two most moving and instructive passages in his career. I like the historical book, *In the American Grain*, I like much of that very well indeed. The novels have not grabbed me; a few stories. I think he was a major figure in the twentieth century, perhaps in spite of himself.

With your interest in meter and measure, how do you react to Williams' emphasis on measure, on finding an American measure, and his attempts to break a Whitman line into three parts, to put the Whitman line into a proper measure, his creation of the variable foot, and so on?

Well, very simply and with great respect for Williams, it's this: that his theories about meter are interesting because he writes meters, not because he writes *about* meters. I think that he writes, when he writes critically, too confusingly, too vaguely, which he does not do when he's writing poems.

The direct influence of Williams on your work would be seen in "American Sketches"?

I was trying to perform a sort of *hommage* to Williams there, but I wouldn't be surprised if I could show . . .

I would think in these snapshotlike pieces, too.

Maybe. What I think happens is that, say, X turns something up, but it really doesn't belong to him or her; it's something that's in the culture, and you are free to deal with it, to try your hand at it too, I think, without becoming an epigone. Now there have been epigones of Williams, but that's a different story.

You wouldn't be mistaken for one of those.

To tell the truth, I don't think that he would have liked me, but that doesn't matter.

He's the one of that generation you read the most?

If I'm looking to learn something, yes, and next to him Stevens. Stevens would be a close second. They are very different, even though they were friends of a sort.

Marianne Moore?

I read her, but I prefer Elizabeth Bishop. I would think that Elizabeth Bishop is Marianne Moore perfected. On the other hand, something must be said for Moore because she was in this vein the pioneer. I like reading them both actually, but seeing things historically is important, I believe, for the writer. I have students who don't think so, who think everything was all written at the same time, usually yesterday. I think it is interesting to know that Elizabeth Bishop comes after Marianne Moore, if only for the sake of accuracy and historical truth. But also for the evolution of an art; the changes, aside from their intrinsic interest, cannot fail to show you something about your own work if you're willing to learn.

That brings us back to Selected Poems *and why it's in "fair chronological order."*

Well, I did some things after other writers and some things before other writers and this ought to lay out the record of which was which. For those who care.

(1980)

*Some Poems Mentioned
in the Interviews*

Portrait with Short Hair

The days, the days!
And the scissors you cut
Your hair with—oh, how dull.
Time to change the needle.

Put on another record—
No, something baroque—
And think of the good times.
Think of lakes and rivers.

It's hot. Let in some air.
Let the smell of leftovers
Be one with the perfume
Of cooling asphalt, leaves.

And the nights? Ah, wonderful—
You alone,
Alone with the slums,
The flowerpots, the stars.

Think of the sea. Unzip,
Just as though someone were
Around to be made love to,
Or anyway to pose for.

The mysteries of sex!
Some day you'll wake up
Back on that Christmas morning
In Mexico, still a virgin.

From "Portraits of the Sixties."

To the Hawks

McNamara, Rusk, Bundy, etc.

Farewell is the bell
Beginning to ring.

The children singing
Do not yet hear it.

The sun is shining
In their song. The sun

Is in fact shining
Upon the schoolyard,

On children swinging
Like tongues of a bell

Swung out on the long
Arc of a silence

That will not seem to
Have been a silence

Till it is broken,
As it is breaking.

There is a sun now
Louder than the sun

Of which the children
Are singing, brighter,

Too, than that other
Against whose brightness

Their eyes seem caught in
The act of shutting.

The young schoolteacher,
Waving one arm in

Time to the music,
Is waving farewell.

Her mouth is open
To sound the alarm.

The mouth of the world
Grows round with the sound.

February, 1965

Men at Forty

Men at forty
Learn to close softly
The doors to rooms they will not be
Coming back to.

At rest on a stair landing,
They feel it
Moving beneath them now like the deck of a ship,
Though the swell is gentle.

And deep in mirrors
They rediscover
The face of the boy as he practices tying
His father's tie there in secret

And the face of that father,
Still warm with the mystery of lather.
They are more fathers than sons themselves now.
Something is filling them, something

That is like the twilight sound
Of the crickets, immense,
Filling the woods at the foot of the slope
Behind their mortgaged houses.

Sestina: Here in Katmandu

We have climbed the mountain.
There's nothing more to do.
It is terrible to come down
To the valley
Where, amidst many flowers,
One thinks of snow,

As formerly, amidst snow,
Climbing the mountain,
One thought of flowers,
Tremulous, ruddy with dew,
In the valley.
One caught their scent coming down.

It is difficult to adjust, once down,
To the absence of snow.
Clear days, from the valley,
One looks up at the mountain.
What else is there to do?
Prayer wheels, flowers!

Let the flowers
Fade, the prayer wheels run down.
What have they to do
With us who have stood atop the snow
Atop the mountain,
Flags seen from the valley?

It might be possible to live in the valley,
To bury oneself among flowers,
If one could forget the mountain,
How, never once looking down,
Stiff, blinded with snow,
One knew what to do.

Meanwhile it is not easy here in Katmandu,
Especially when to the valley
That wind which means snow
Elsewhere, but here means flowers,
Comes down,
As soon it must, from the mountain.

The Assassination

It begins again, the nocturnal pulse.
It courses through the cables laid for it.
It mounts to the chandeliers and beats there, hotly.
We are too close. Too late, we would move back.
We are involved with the surge.

Now it bursts. Now it has been announced.
Now it is being soaked up by newspapers.
Now it is running through the streets.
The crowd has it. The woman selling carnations
And the man in the straw hat stand with it in their shoes.

Here is the red marquee it sheltered under,
Here is the ballroom, here
The sadly various orchestra led
By a single gesture. My arms open.
It enters. Look, we are dancing.

June 5, 1968

5

There is a word for it,
A simple word,
And the word goes around.

It curves like a staircase,
And it goes up like a staircase,
And it *is* a staircase,

An iron staircase
On the side of a lighthouse.
All in his head.

And it makes no sound at all
In his head,
Unless he says it.

Then the keeper
Steps on the rung,
The bottom rung,

And the ascent begins.
Clangorous,
Rung after rung.

He wants to keep the light going,
If he can.

But the man closing up
Does not say the word.

From "The Man Closing Up."

From "Childhood"

All day

There is a smell of ocean longing landward.
And, high on his frail ladder, my father
Stands hammering great storm shutters down
Across the windows of the tall hotels,
Swaying. Around downed wires, across broken fronds,
Our Essex steers, bargelike and slow . . .
    Westward now,
The smoky rose of oblivion blooms, hangs;
And on my knee a small red sun-glow, setting.
For a long time I feel, coming and going in waves,
The stupid wish to cry. I dream . . .

the hurricane season

obsolete make of car

the Everglades on fire
my osteomyelitis—anesthesias

123

Cool Dark Ode

You could have sneaked up,
Broken into those underheated rooms
By the windows overlooking the tavern,
Or the back way, up the broad but unlighted stairs,
At a moment when no one was present,
When the long planed table that served as a desk
Was recalling the quiet of the woods,
When the books, older, were thinking farther back,
To the same essential stillness,
And both table and books, if they thought of the future
     ever,
Probably shuddered, as though from a stray draft,
Seeing themselves as eventual flame,
Some final smoke.

Now, when there is no longer any occasion,
I think of inviting you in
To wait for us
On the short, cramped sofa,
Beside the single candle-stub,
Which must have frightened you off then,
Or in the cubicle of the bedroom,
Where even then we imagined ourselves extinguished
By your total embrace,
Attentive meanwhile to the animal noises of your breathing,
The whimpers,
The sudden intoxicated outcries,
That were not our own.

Night, night, O blackness of winter,
I tell you this, you
That used to come up as far as the frosted panes, the door,
As far as the edges of our skin,

From "Three Odes."

Without any thought, I know now,
Of entering those borrowed rooms,
Or even our mouths, our eyes,
Which all too often were carelessly left open for you.

Landscape with Little Figures

There were some pines, a canal, a piece of sky.
The pines are the houses now of the very poor,
Huddled together, in a blue, ragged wind.
Children go whistling their dogs, down by the mudflats,
Once the canal. There's a red ball lost in the weeds.
It's winter, it's after supper, it's goodbye.
O goodbye to the houses, the children, the little red ball,
And the pieces of sky that will go on falling for days.

Sonatina in Yellow

Du schnell vergehendes Daguerrotyp
In meinen langsamer vergehenden Händen.

—*Rilke*

The pages of the album,
As they are turned, turn yellow; a word,
Once spoken, obsolete,
No longer what was meant. Say it.
The meanings come, or come back later,
Unobtrusive, taking their places.

Think of the past. Think of forgetting the past.
It was an exercise requiring further practice;
A difficult exercise, played through by someone else.
Overheard from another room, now,
It seems full of mistakes.
                              So the voice of your father,
Rising as from the next room still
With all the remote but true affection of the dead,
Repeats itself, insists,
Insisting you must listen, rises
In the familiar pattern of reproof
For some childish error, a nap disturbed,
Or vase, broken or overturned;
Rises and subsides. And you do listen.
Listen and forget. Practice forgetting.

Forgotten sunlight still
Blinds the eyes of faces in the album.
The faces fade, and there is only
A sort of meaning that comes back,
Or for the first time comes, but comes too late
To take the places of the faces.

                              Remember
The dead air of summer. Remember
The trees drawn up to their full height like fathers,

The underworld of shade you entered at their feet.
Enter the next room. Enter it quietly now,
Not to disturb your father sleeping there. *He stirs.*
Notice his clothes, how scrupulously clean,
Unwrinkled from the nap; his face, freckled with work,
Smoothed by a passing dream. The vase
Is not yet broken, the still young roses
Drink there from perpetual waters. *He rises, speaks . . .*

Repeat it now, no one was listening.
So your hand moves, moving across the keys,
And slowly the keys grow darker to the touch.

Mule Team and Poster

Two mules stand waiting in front of the brick wall of a warehouse,
>hitched to a shabby flatbed wagon.
Its spoked wheels resemble crude wooden flowers
>pulled recently from a deep and stubborn mud.

The rains have passed over for now,
>and the sun is back,
Invisible but everywhere present,
>and of a special brightness, like God.

The way the poster for the traveling show
>still clings to its section of the wall
It looks as though a huge door stood open
>or a terrible flap of brain had been peeled
>>back, revealing

Someone's idea of heaven:
>seven dancing girls, caught on the up-kick,
All in fringed dresses and bobbed hair.
>One wears a Spanish comb and has an escort . . .

Meanwhile the mules crunch patiently the few cornshucks
>someone has patiently scattered for them.
The poster is torn in places, slightly crumpled;
>a few bricks, here and there, show through.

And a long shadow—
>the last shade perhaps in all of Alabama—
Stretches beneath the wagon, crookedly,
>like a great scythe laid down there and forgotten.

—on a photograph by Walker Evans (Alabama, 1936)

II

Notes of an Outsider

Notes of an Outsider

The Tearstain Test

According to Thomas Moore, the manuscript of one of Byron's poems written to the wife he had separated from, with great scandal, was "blotted all over with the marks of tears." Years later, when the original draft was offered at auction, Ernest Hartley Coleridge had a chance to examine the manuscript. To his great disappointment he could find no tearstains at all.

Question: Would the poem have been any better had he found tearstains?

A Personal Note

> The leaves are falling; so am I. (Landor)

Here the note of the personal merges with and becomes inseparable from the impersonal convention.

Generations later, same theme:

> Rotting Ginsberg, I stared in the mirror naked today
> I noticed the old skull, I'm getting balder
> my pate gleams, etc.

Here whatever of the impersonal was left in the theme has been swallowed up in the merely personal. It is probably funnier than intended.

How to Manufacture an Image

In Prinzhorn's book on the paintings of the mad a patient is quoted: "The head is made up of a 42 cm. shell [the largest German shell of WWI] which turns into a Papal tiara and finally into a magnificent pile of straw." Would anyone be surprised to find in a poem published tomorrow a line running something like this?—"the explosive head, a tiara, a pile of straw." Or more strictly in the current manner: "the head exploding like a tiara of straw." If anything, it makes almost too much sense.

The Wild Garden

Organic form as a doctrine seems to demand an almost religious act of assent, and as a doctrine it has won almost universal acceptance in our superannuated Romantic age. It seems to imply, vaguely—and I have always found it vague as well as evangelical—that, in poetry, that poem will be best which springs up naturally, rather like a flower, I suppose, or a weed. And without any acknowledged necessity for preparing the ground with tools, for enriching it with fertilizer, for judicious pruning, clipping, or grafting. The result is a flower—I mean a poem—which will bear witness to its own naturalness, its organic character, just by virtue of the absence of all marks reflecting similitude and kind, marks such as symmetry, repetitive and predictive numerical features or patterns (such as the leaves of trees and bushes, for example) by means of which in the botanical world we identify genus and species. In short, the poems growing out of such a doctrine are less likely to bear marks of the generic than of the individual, since each is ideally a species unto itself, without kin—and therefore in this way quite against nature. Imagine the chaos of such a garden, the mad variety of so wide a field!

An afterthought: the organicist wishes to assert a beguiling but false claim to identity with something beyond or other than himself, to become, as it were, another of the non-human but sometimes expressive voices of nature, like the very thunder, say.

A Case of Translating Oneself

A minor literary curiosity: two versions of the same little epigram, one in English, one in French, and I cannot tell which is the original, which the translation. What makes it a curiosity is that the same author—Landor—wrote both.

> Ye walls! sole witnesses of happy sighs,
>> Say not, blest walls, one word.
> Remember, but keep safe from ears and eyes
>> All you have seen and heard.

> *O murs! temoins des plus heureux soupirs,*
> *N'en dites mot: gardez nos souvenirs.*

Probably the English version came first, since English was Landor's native tongue, yet I happen to prefer here the "translation," if that is what it is.

The case does suggest to me that the same "content"—not precisely the same, but very, very close—may be carried by structures (forms?) very different, different in important ways.

The Economical Version

Landor again.

> Ternissa! you are fled!
> I say not to the dead,
> But to the happy ones who rest below:
>> For surely, surely where
>> Your voice and graces are
> Nothing of death can any feel or know.
>> Girls who delight to dwell
>> Where grows most asphodel
> Gather to their calm breasts each word you speak:
>> The mild Persephone
>> Places you on her knee,
> And your cool palm smooths down stern Pluto's cheek.

I find this very beautiful, and a part of its beauty, at least for me, is its great brevity. Yet I am pretty sure that I spot evidences of padding. Let's see what happens if I cut each line down by one metrical foot.

> You are not fled
> Unto the dead
> But to the happy ones below:
> For surely where
> Your graces are
> Nothing of death can any know.
> Now they who dwell
> With asphodel
> Grow calmer with each word you speak:
> Persephone
> Upon her knee
> Takes you, to smooth stern Pluto's cheek.

Essentially the same argument, still recognizably the Landor style. My wild guess is that the poem was originally written in lines like these, of two and four feet, down to the last line, which turned out to require an extra foot—and turned out so well as a pentameter that the poet cheerfully rewrote the poem backwards, so to speak, padding skillfully along the way, and all for the sake, at least to start with, of the slow and stately Pluto line.

The true version is clearly superior to my reduction, suggesting, among other things, that the severest economy is not always in the interest of beauty and expressiveness. The point is obvious enough, though I have heard it argued the other way, to my astonishment. (The teacher, for instance, who urged his students to drop all articles from their poems in the interest of economy.)

No predetermined meter seems to have been essential here. What seemed to count was a series of small, nice, tactful accommodations of phrase, line, and argument to one another, a sort of moment-to-moment feeling out of the way very much like what occurs in the writing of most free verse. The lines were tested not against a measure or limit fixed and specified in advance—which is what the anti-traditionalist automatically finds himself claiming—but against the very idea of measure itself. What was called for was not an *exact* measure, but *an* exact measure.

The Visiting Critic

We were so appalled by the lecture—one of those in the provinces for which the distinguished lecturer has failed to make adequate preparation—that we did not go to the party afterward.

Looking over my notes I find that he seems to have said at one point, "Words like meanings are somehow cut loose from one another." He may have said *feelings* or meant *feelings* rather than *meanings*, but from his alcohol-slurred speech I could only gather *meanings*. Perhaps it hardly matters, for once these are cut loose, whatever they are, they seem to "whirl around in a flurry" within a—I did not quite catch what the lecturer said here but I think it was the *void*, if the void has flurries. The void, I suppose, hath no flurry like a meaning spurned.

Also I heard, endlessly repeated—rather like the image of the ocean spliced into that camp classic, *The Loves of Isadora*, in order to patch over the numerous gaps in continuity—the abominable catch phrase, *Syntax is bogus!* This, mind you, in a fairly passable syntax, given the rather improvisational character of the critic's remarks. Presumably he meant that syntax was bogus for the "modernist" spirit in literature. Well, that is simply not so. It's bogus perhaps for some disturbed patients, for some children, for some poets even. Alas. And for some literary critics, although not so much in their own speech and writing as in what they read and choose to praise.

In any case, an orderly syntax is not equivalent—as this critic claimed—to believing that the world itself possesses an order, certainly not a benign order. I employ syntax even now to disclaim such a faith.

Little Ossians

One side effect of an age of translation like ours is that the image is elevated to a role of supreme importance in our native poetry, since the image proves far easier to translate than, say, the rhythms of the original. It is as if our American poets, upon reading Homer, had all become little Ossians. It is as if poetry were now written in an international language, like music, but unfortunately not musical.

Self-hatred in the Academy

Critics tend to feel comfortable with a poetry of ideas—that is, explicit ideas. It gives them something to talk about.

Failing ideas, look for critics to fall for the avant-garde. Best, of course, when the two are combined, as in the work of Charles Olson. I mean that department of the avant-garde— the largest, perhaps—whose works are notable chiefly for being practical demonstrations of a theory. Are we back to ideas after all? Academic critics in particular seem susceptible. How many in the academies bravely espouse the avant-garde, especially yesteryear's! Olson, again . . .

This happens to be true of academic critics of new fiction as well. The darlings of this set are the so-called experimentalists. Why this should have come to pass in the last decade or so I cannot guess, but it was not always so. On the contrary, when I was a student, oh, distressingly to the contrary. But the pendulum has swung too violently back in the other direction now, and I can only suggest a sociological term to account for it: self-hate. Paradox: the academic critic scorns any new work which does not attack the academy!

Platonic Scripts

I write or try to write as if convinced that, prior to my attempt, there existed a true text, a sort of Platonic script, which I had been elected to transcribe or record.

Where Did Free Verse Come From

Free verse in long lines has been thought to come from the King James Bible and Walt Whitman, at least in English. Possibly in other European languages something of the same thing may hold, though I am not sure. I think, for instance, of Laforgue's translations of Whitman in 1886 for Gustav Kahn's

La Vogue—just about the time *vers libre* was being defined, indeed actually invented, in French. To this as a source I think we ought to add the classic blank-verse line, and perhaps by extension the standard heroic line of the other languages. Looking at Apollinaire's "Zone," for example, one still finds many alexandrines, often with the caesura displaced, a sort of mobile caesura, which tends to weaken the traditional character of the twelve-syllable line (*vers libéré*). In Eliot's early verse also this "memory" of the past continues, but brokenly, and here and there whole lines of blank verse remain intact (as in "Mr. Apollinax").

But what of free verse in short lines? In French, in some of the "Choses" by Guillevic, for example, it seems one can quite plainly see—and hear—bits and pieces of alexandrines, often halves or thirds in a row, making up whole twelve-syllable groups, and this to such an extent as to make for an apparent if erratic patterning. If this is so—and taking the possibility as a clue—one may suppose that the short line in English (which is to say, American) free verse came originally from a breaking up of the old blank-verse line, conscious or not, into smaller, varying units. Considering only the accents in a good deal of this early free verse, we find the lines turning out to vary usually between two and three accents—that is, the old heroic line broken into two almost equivalent pieces. This possibility ought to be added to the more familiar suggestion that such a line stems historically from the practice of the Imagists, H.D. in particular.

Pages from Unwritten Books

Some poems these days resemble those passages in novels where the narrative slows or ceases, allowing the hero time to reflect or to reach some sort of psychological conclusion or moral decision. With this vast difference, however—that in the novel there is an amplitude of context and we are expected to be acquainted with a certain background the novelist has conscientiously provided, to recognize references to details of setting, other characters, events that have gone before, etc., whereas in the type of poem I am thinking of we are likely to be deprived of any recognizable and knowable context. It is as if so much of what in a novel gives us that sense of the wholeness of life had been drained away, as well as the pleasures of recognition and the privileges of understanding, leaving only a sort of pure and rarefied psychological essence for contemplation. The rather elementary form of mysteriousness which results is distinctly not an advantage, though perhaps confused with true mystery and therefore praised by some.

Thus many poems these days read like incomplete novels—pages torn from lost or unwritten books.

There is perhaps a little more to be said about the sheer *prose* of poems now. The secrets of the rhythms of free verse seem to have been lost to nearly a whole generation. It is as if the old and young had been playing a game of Gossip—in which the whispered "secrets," being passed on, had undergone curious warpings. Or are poets just not interested anymore?

Measure
Measure objectifies.

On Mumbling in Poetry
The Actor's Studio style of acting—popular in the forties and fifties, and represented vividly still in my mind by Brando's performance in *Streetcar*—was the antithesis of everything British on stage. Mumbles, grunts, scratches. This style became accepted as a theatrical means of *imitating* natural behavior and a certain sincerity. It was opposed to an earlier theory of eloquence, according to which the actor in his role was expected to speak at a higher pitch of emotion nowhere more than just before his heroic death, as it might be. So with Othello on the point of death, as Eliot for one has pointed out. And this surely would have been understood—note the acceptance in law of deathbed testimony—as the moment of greatest "sincerity" as well. Now, however, sincerity is thought to be proved by little more than an inability to articulate. If the emotion which finds expression in whole and well-round-

ed sentences becomes suspect, what then of the verse of Shakespeare?

There may be an analogy to this in the decay of meters after WWII. As the Actor's Studio style swept the country, so did various types of free verse. (Anti-British, too, of course, under the banner of Dr. Williams.) Mumbles and grunts? Well, sometimes it does seem that way. I like it myself, for certain things; no denying its interest, its appropriateness on occasion, the welcome relief of such deflations. But taken as the very sign of the sincere and deeply felt? Spare me the paradox.

The Dying Pleasures of Movie Criticism

I realize now that one of the reasons my serious interest in the movies—a lifelong passion, really (which probably dates back to watching *The Jazz Singer* from my mother's knee)— revived in the late sixties was that I began to read film criticism, not professionally but casually, for pleasure. I was no longer able to find so pure and uncompromised a pleasure in reading literary criticism, which in adolescence I had often been actually thrilled by. Some of it had been damned good, in fact. Now I was bored and in some cases actively offended by it; it seemed vague and to me quite irrelevant (by which I mean that it talked about things that as a writer I never thought of or acted on). The literary review was showing less and less of a sense of history (even of recent history). Received opinions developed instantly, were held unanimously, and remained unexamined. Worst of all perhaps, there was a dreadful party spirit abroad. Reviewers had always puffed their friends (Jarrell on early Lowell) and picked fights with enemies, real or imaginary. And I know that there must always have been and always will be a certain amount of propagandizing and browbeating, but one may be excused all the same for growing weary of the pronunciamentos of a Bly or the personal unpleasantness of the *Georgia Review* houseman or the condescensions of unfledged Ivy Leaguers in *Poetry*.

Movie criticism seemed an altogether happier realm to escape to. Even the reviewers seemed to love their work and treated the movies—at least the movies of the past, including honorable failures—with affection and respect. Furthermore, they delighted in acquiring a great deal of information about what they were writing of and in putting that information to work for them. None of this was any longer true of the reviewers of new poetry or, with an exception or two, of the handful who over the next decade were to attempt books on the subject. I have made the experiment of interchanging the praise for poem A with the disdain for poem B expressed by the same reviewer in the same review; I could not see that one was more appropriate or fair than the other. An interchangeable criticism for interchangeable poems!

But of late structuralism—the dead hand of the academy—has touched even movie criticism. And even a reviewer for the popular press like Pauline Kael sounds as shrill as if she were reviewing poetry. Gary Arnold and Andrew Sarris are exceptions still, I think. But on the whole movie criticism is just no fun anymore.

Yet I seem to need a little criticism mixed into my general reading diet, and lately I find myself dipping into art criticism, in which thankfully I do not yet know my way. I do find it comforting that the art critics and reviewers seem to have looked at the pictures first and to be capable of describing them and making distinctions among them, sometimes even commenting on technical matters far beyond me but of great interest all the same. It's refreshing. I am strangely encouraged to look at pictures myself. Oh, I already see party spirit here, uninformed though I am, but, as I say, that does seem always to be around the fringes of the arts. If art criticism should eventually fail me, I may have to settle in the end for the criticism of rock music. What my son tells me of that sounds promising.

On Line Lengths

One day in the early sixties, calling on my friend Mark Strand, I noticed in his typewriter a piece of paper on which a poem was apparently being revised. Other people's revisions always have a mysterious look about them, and I asked exactly what he was trying to do. The reply was that he was trying to get the lines to come out "even," all about the same length, so that they would look right.

However obvious this notion may seem to others it had never occurred to me before. In any case, I immediately saw the point and considered that I had learned something.

Seven or eight years later, calling again on the same poet, I noticed in the same typewriter a new poem, also apparently being revised, but with quite a different look about it even so. I found myself asking the same question as before, but this time the reply was not the same. It seems he was trying to *keep* the lines from coming out even!

This was my second lesson.

I suppose there must be a third.

(1962–1982)

Baudelaire

The Question of His Sincerity; or, Variations on Several Texts by Eliot

Before Adam ate of the fruit which made him a poet and hence an exile, not even the serpent could have questioned his sincerity. The term is inapplicable to a state of innocence.

It may be inapplicable today, though for just the opposite reason. For if sincerity is a critical measure at all, it must certainly be one of the most primitive. It follows (to extend the fable) immediately upon the fall: it was the sincerity of Cain which was in question. Nevertheless the issue of sincerity is a durable one; somehow it survives, in undergraduate essay and newspaper review, in the dark corners of the literary cellar. We who have left behind both the innocent state where sincerity is not even an issue and the primitive state where it is virtually the only one, do not like to raise the question, at least not in public. Yet it is this very question which, I suspect, drives the critic at last to desperate measures—to biography. For sincerity, conceived on this elementary plane, means not only *believing what you say* but *acting out in your life what you say in your poetry, and preferably before writing it down.* Sooner or later the writer who follows such a course wins the moral approbation of his audience, for it is obviously wrong, though appallingly human, to say or do what you do not believe. The poems he writes are likely to be confessional in tone: the heart laid bare. Since there can be no reason for concealing one's honorable daytime nature, it becomes a special mark of value, a test of *real* sincerity, if one can confess to those dreadful nighttime imaginings characteristic, apparently, of the latter stages of Romanticism. Hence those orgies of public confession or self-expression—vulgarly known as "getting it out of your system"—upon which absolution, or perhaps merely health, is expected to follow. Such, at any rate, is the poetry which receives the title "sincere."*

Now I have not yet, I think, described the poetry of Baudelaire, though it may seem that I have tried to do so.

Most of us would agree, in any case, that one of the grounds of Baudelaire's permanent popularity involves a misconception of his role, and it is just here that the question of sincerity, of what kind of sincerity we are talking about, becomes important. Did he describe a naked, dancing black Venus?

> La très-chère etait nue, et, connaissant mon coeur,
> Elle n'avait gardé que ses bijoux sonores,
> Dont le riche attirail lui donnait l'air vainqueur
> Qu'ont dans leurs jours heureux les esclaves des Mores.

> My beloved was naked, and, knowing my heart,
> She wore nothing but her tinkling jewelry,
> Whose rich show gave her the conquering air
> Moorish slaves have, during their happy days.

We are reassured that he did actually keep such a mistress. Did he describe a woman painting her bosom at the mirror?

> —"Je vois ta mère, enfant de ce siècle appauvri,
> Qui vers son miroir penche un lourd amas d'années,
> Et plâtre artistement le sein qui t'a nourri!"

> "I see your mother, child of this impoverished age,
> Bent by a heavy weight of years towards her mirror,
> And artfully painting the bosom which nursed you!"

We are told that his mother probably so adorned herself in the early days with the general. Is his art, on the whole, dol-

---

*I am mildly surprised to find myself raising this question before, though not much before, the first "confessional" texts of our period, Lowell's and Snodgrass', saw the light.

orous? Luckily, for his reputation for sincerity, his life was equally so. Thus the case is proved, by means of what I call the biographical test of sincerity.

The texts from Eliot provide a surprising example of the extent to which such a test is honored, in high quarters as well as low. The first reads: "In his verse [Baudelaire] is now less a model to be imitated or a source to be drained than a reminder of the duty, the consecrated task, of sincerity." The second, which serves to gloss the first, is: "The best that can be said [for Baudelaire], and that is a very great deal, is that what he knew he found out for himself."

Sincerity so conceived, as a kind of equation between the life and the work, seems to me possibly not a measure of literature at all. On the other hand, it might do as a workable standard for life. But we can scarcely afford to exchange criticism for ethics.

The value of such sincerity in art is easily recognizable as a market value. It leads, among other things, to interesting portraits of the author on book jackets, to illustrations, perhaps, by Beardsley. It is not hard to imagine the writer, once he has discovered this rather simple fact, *choosing* to be sincere as he sharpens the pencil which will dash off the hundred alexandrines for the day.

Sincerity may be a pose, then; a pose which amounts to the poet's *saying what other people believe.* Of course the writer may happen to believe it too. He probably must, if he is going to cash in.

But to say that sincerity is a pose provides only the first of two propositions, of which the second is: *A pose may be sincere.*

It is by means of this second proposition that we approach a revised definition of the sincerity which matters, not in life but in art. Sincerity is *saying what the form obliges you to say regardless of whether or not you believe in it.** A more humane version of this, one which has been proposed by several modern critics in other contexts, is *discovering what you mean by or in*

---

*Of course, once you have said it, you ought to be willing to espouse what you have felt obliged to say—or to keep decently silent.

the act of saying it. The poet—the sincere poet—becomes a performer, a charlatan, a great pretender; art is artifice. What he has to be sincere about is his art. The idea of the depersonalization of the artist—appropriated by Eliot from the French—seems to be a by-product of this attitude. At last it would appear that the private life of the poet has ceased to matter.

And Baudelaire ought to have emerged before now as a great exemplar of this kind of sincerity. To a degree, he has.

But as it was Baudelaire's misfortune to be a pioneer of the new attitude, of the pose which is a form of sincerity, he seems to have felt obliged to be sincere in the more primitive sense as well, to carry the experiment of his art over into his own life, in short, using the terms I have adopted, to apply the biographical test to his own work. I hesitate to ponder on the degree of consciousness and deliberation involved in this choice. But here we have one means of accounting for the elegant English costume, the experiments with hashish, and so on; as against the obvious counterexplanation that he carried his experiments in life over into his art it has the advantage of treating the work as primary, the life as secondary.

Baudelaire himself seems to have conceived of his role somewhat in this fashion. In a note accompanying one of the more or less blasphemous groups of poems he wrote: *"Fidèle a son douloureux programme, l'auteur des* Fleurs du Mal *a dû, en parfait comédien, façonner son esprit a tous les sophismes comme à toutes les corruptions."* The pose obliged him to adopt those notorious paraphernalia of decadence which, according to Eliot, "have not worn very well." But all of this—"his prostitutes, mulattoes, Jewesses, serpents, cats, corpses"—Eliot hastens to add, was "hardly more than an accident of the time," assuming, and I think rightly, that at another time Baudelaire's pose might well have been constituted of shepherdesses and oaten pipes. The important point is that the paraphernalia were an aspect of the pose, fashionable, of course, but more or less a product of the deliberate will. Coupled with the paraphernalia is that high moral tone which might seem, except for the example of Baudelaire, so incompatible with the subject matter. Neither is new; it is their union which produces the *frisson nouveau* on which Hugo congratulated the poet. But how are we to disentangle the one aspect of the *frisson* from the other? How are we, in other words, to claim that here, in the high moral tone, Baudelaire was sincere; and in the other, the paraphernalia of decadence, he was not? Only, it seems to me, by the application of the biographical test, by extracting comments from the reminiscence of the right sort of friend, by piecing together fragments from the letters and the journals, especially from the later ones when he had already written most of the poems. My suggestion is that both are parts of the same pose and that both are equally "sincere" in respect to his art. Decadence alone was not enough; neither was the high moral tone; it was the combination of the two which made up the pose to whose discoveries he was faithful. Whether or not he "believed" in them is another matter.

(1957)

The Private History of a Poem

A poet tends as a matter of course to some narcissism about his work. Why otherwise should he keep about him these bundles of old worksheets but in the dwindling hope that some line rejected from the old poem, for reasons excellent enough, no doubt, may be rescued for the new? Why, indeed, should he be tempted to set down an account of the composition of one of his poems? I sometimes suspect that all such accounts, from Poe through Jarrell, stem from nothing more than a mere innocent affection for the first idea of the poem, that pure and as yet uncompromised conception which somehow shrinks and becomes disfigured in the writing; or perhaps only for some portion of an early draft now gone, one with which the poet is reluctant to part without a backward look. I myself am not sure that I would take as much pleasure in writing were it possible to commit the original idea with perfect spontaneity to paper, nor am I at all sure that such poems would be as interesting as one might like to believe in the midst of the long night of labor. Even so it is true, at least in my own experience, that the conception of a poem does usually in some respect seem more impressive, grander, than the finished product, which almost always represents a series of compromises between desire and necessity. Even one of my shortest poems—a mere six lines long—started out to be a very long poem, the scraps no doubt still in a box somewhere.

Something like this was true of "Anonymous Drawing," I know. My wife and I had gone to an office in midtown Manhattan to look at a design proposed for the cover of my first book of poems. The design proved to be an altered copy of what I remember now as a drawing by a late Renaissance Italian of no particular fame. I was shown first the mocked-up copy and then, in an anthology of drawings of the period, a reproduction of the original. Several details had been changed slightly and the whole design "flopped over." The question of what connection this drawing—pleasing as it might be in itself—could have with the poems in the book troubled me from the start. Had the details been altered so as to conform to something the designer saw in the poems, provided of course that he had read them? Did poems and drawing both seem Southern perhaps? Ornamental? Old-fashioned? Hoping that none of these was the answer, I nevertheless felt a certain strangeness about my own poems, since someone else had apparently seen in them—and in the drawing—what I could not.

Somewhere in this experience lay a poem, although not until the first few lines occurred to me during the uneventful ride in the subway back to our hotel did I become aware of this as a distinct possibility.

> This young Negro whose nose
> The designer for God knows
> What queer reasons of love or hate
> Has made straight

These lines came, as seems most often to be the case, without deliberate effort, indeed with hardly a conscious thought that I might be beginning a poem; and to these lines, optimistically enough, I immediately gave the title, "On the Cover Design for My First Book." Before we had arrived at the hotel I had determined to finish it in time for inclusion in that book, which was going to be a rather small collection at best.

Anyone who has looked at *The Summer Anniversaries* will realize that the poem was not included there and that this was not the cover design. The book, for various complicated reasons, found a different publisher; another design was done; and I did not write the poem. Before we left New York a few days later I had added only one line and decided on a possible rhyme for the next.

> Stands with the reins of a horse
> . . . . of course

Nevertheless I felt that here was a promising beginning. Let me explain at once what I mean by this immodesty. Often at the outset of a poem, when the first few lines have been drafted, the most pressing problem for me becomes what I think of as "discovering the form." What meters will the poem have? What rhymes, and what sort, if any? What tone will it take?—a question involving diction and imagery as well. If the more or less "given" lines answer these questions for me, it is, in this sense, a promising beginning. And this handful of lines answered most of these questions: the meters would be more or less free and the lines of varying lengths, but as if by way of compensation each pair of lines would be strictly rhymed. If this much of the form, by some wild chance, resembled Ogden Nash, then the tone would have to speak for the difference.

However promising the beginning may have seemed I could not get any farther. I worked on other poems. When I returned to this one, a year had passed. I had not set the lines down in a notebook, but neither had I forgotten them, nor indeed the whole train of questions the drawing had raised for me. What I had forgotten was the name of the artist; he might have been anonymous for all I could remember. I had studied the drawing for two minutes at most, and now its details had begun to slip from memory. Although the book was to be brought out by a different publisher, I wrote the first publisher asking for the name of the artist so that I might look the drawing up. But he could not remember, and the designer himself had, if I remember correctly, been drafted. Hearing this, I spent several futile afternoons thumbing through the collections in the local art library. The drawing was not to be found.

Again I laid the poem aside, but this time with the precaution of writing down the first five lines, without having added a word, and now with little expectation of turning up the drawing which would, I had begun to feel, enable me at one stroke to finish the poem.

When next I took up these lines, early in 1961, a little more than two years had passed since the subway ride. I finished the sixth line now:

> Clutched in one hand—still black, of course

Not long after this very small but to me encouraging progress I was asked to contribute a poem on the subject of the imagination to a booklet of poems on that subject soon to be printed. Although I had another poem underway that happened to deal with this theme, as a hedge against failure with that one, I kept returning, in the intervals of work on it, to the poem I had grown to think of as "On an Abandoned Cover Design for My First Book." That book had now been out for a year, by the way. Curiously enough, the need to see the original drawing had passed and, with its passing, work on the poem went much more easily.

> But delicately molded
> Like the wings of a butterfly when they are folded.
> So delicate, indeed, is this boy in every feature
> That one questions whether he can hold the spirited
>   creature
>   Beside him
> Until the master shall arrive to ride him.

From there I skipped to the end, being unable to flatter myself that I actually remembered the details of the drawing. And probably I sensed that with the mention of "the master" I had arrived at the real center of the poem, at the moment an intuitive recognition only, and one I had better not hurry. Meanwhile I would try to get down the feelings the first sight of the design had aroused regarding my poems.

And since it is meant to accompany my book,
I study the design; I look
But am puzzled and cannot establish
Any connection between this lie and the lies I publish,
    Unless it be only
That it pictures a world for which, in weak moments, all
      of us grow lonely,
    That, just as my poems said,
This world so pretty and privileged is dead
And could not have lasted very much longer anyway.
The master has long since arrived and ridden away.

That seemed to put the case clearly enough, but very roughly and all too openly, except for the last line. (That is the line I most regret.) But with this last line I was more than ever convinced that "the master" would have to be at the center of the poem. I think I must have associated this absent personage vaguely with what a Freudian might call a "father-figure" (my father being dead), or with God, or with some chivalric hero of the past, or possibly with all of these at once. And if this were true, then the boy might well be myself; the horse, among other things, my "Pegasus"; and the scene, about which more and more wistful feelings were beginning to gather, since it was doubly vanished, might well have been related to childhood, a time of life about which I can easily become sentimental.

However, once such speculations begin, any really immediate work on the poem ceases, or so I find. It was not till a day or two later that I turned to filling in details descriptive of the by-this-time half-imaginary drawing. For this I was able to draw largely on notes jotted down in the intervals of work on beginning and end. (Meanwhile the other poem on "the imagination" had been temporarily—now permanently—abandoned.) Here are two samples of such notes for the same passage:

> The horse, not without spirit, rears,
> Sighting his master as he nears
> Across the greensward which, it is implied,

Stretches as wide
As this summer of the late Renaissance
In which they posed and sweated once
. . . .
The boy smiling, the horse rearing
To see their lordly master nearing,
Ruffled probably and beautifully laced
    (Not to our taste)

With some idea of giving the poem more individual charác-
ter, I began making an effort to lengthen out occasional lines
and get them more relaxed, fuller of detail, and in general
prosier than ordinary lines of verse.

His nostrils aslant with fear,
We imagine him snorting, about to rear,
   Smelling his master near.
Meanwhile the boy, who should know about such things
     better than we,
Stands passive and ornamental in his fantastic livery
   Of ruffles and puffed breeches
Watching the artist rough in his purely preliminary sketches,
While behind them somewhere, out of the picture, the one
     who must have paid
For the whole thing, having been delayed,
   Hurries across the greensward,
   A puffed and petty lord

Here and there a rhyme-word evidently contributed to the
invention of the next descriptive detail: thus, *greensward* and
lord. (In the final draft both words remain, but not as rhymes.)
Two or three more times through, then, and the passage was
finished except for a scattering of minor changes.

Already the horse's nostrils quiver with fear,
But if we imagine him snorting, about to rear,
This boy, who should know about such things better than
    we,
Only stands smiling, passive and ornamental, in his fantastic
    livery

Of ruffles and puffed breeches
Watching the artist as he sketches.
Meanwhile the petty lord who must have paid
For the artist's trip up from Perugia, for the horse, for the
    boy, for the whole thing, in fact, has been delayed;
If he should come hurrying over this vast greensward now,
Mopping his brow
Clear of the sweat of a fine Renaissance morning, it would
    be too late.

All along I had been vaguely aware that the sociological ironies implicit in the original set of lines were being scanted but, as long as I was making progress, this troublesome awareness had been pushed off to a back corner of my mind. Now that the almost final draft had been reached it was hard to find any development at all of this strand of meaning after the first few lines. I regretted its absence severely: a dimension of the poem was gone. But with the mild and familiar despair which accompanied this realization came also the hope that if such ironies had been necessary to the poem I had had in mind, they were probably not necessary to the poem I had very nearly written. The test for this seemed to be whether the opening could be revised in line with the new, smaller compass of the poem. It could:

    This young Negro stands
    Clutching the reins of a horse in both his hands

But this version, since it neglected to mention the altered state of the drawing, freed me from having to refer to the occasion for the alteration—the designing of a cover for a book of poems. In fact, to have referred to the drawing now as a cover design would have violated the unity of attention focused on the drawing itself. Nevertheless I was not willing to give up what seemed to me so much without one more try:

    A friend of a friend found the original of this drawing in a
      book
    And thought, I suppose, as being appropriate to *my* book,

To give it a more Southern look
By flopping the whole thing over on its side,
And thought, I suppose, to hide
Its source
By altering the boy if not the horse.

That seemed to me a mistake. I cannot say exactly why; perhaps it was only too flippant. But if it was wrong, for whatever reason, then the whole ending would have to go. And suddenly, granting this, it seemed to me that for the first time I could see the shape of the poem as a whole. It would be necessary only to connect the parts better, to compress a little, to change a word here and there, and in general to make the tone as consistent as possible with my own now much altered idea. The last lines written, those about the steward and the manservant, were the easiest of all the lines to write except for the first few. The title seemed obvious now, considering the circumstances: "Anonymous Drawing."

(1961)

Anonymous Drawing

A delicate young Negro stands
With the reins of a horse clutched loosely in his hands;
So delicate, indeed, that we wonder if he can hold the
    spirited creature beside him
Until the master shall arrive to ride him.
Already the animal's nostrils widen with rage or fear.
But if we imagine him snorting, about to rear,
This boy, who should know about such things better than we,
Only stands smiling, passive and ornamental, in a fantastic
    livery
Of ruffles and puffed breeches,
Watching the artist, apparently, as he sketches.
Meanwhile the petty lord who must have paid
For the artist's trip up from Perugia, for the horse, for the
    boy, for everything here, in fact, has been delayed,
Kept too long by his steward, perhaps, discussing

Some business concerning the estate, or fussing
Over the details of his impeccable toilet
With a manservant whose opinion is that any alteration at all
would spoil it.
However fast he should come hurrying now
Over this vast greensward, mopping his brow
Clear of the sweat of this fine Renaissance morning, it would
be too late.
The artist will have had his revenge for being made to wait,
A revenge not only necessary but right and clever—
Simply to leave him out of the scene forever.

On Writing "First Death"

First Death

June 12, 1933

I saw my grandmother grow weak.
When she died, I kissed her cheek.

I remember the new taste—
Powder mixed with a drying paste.

Down the hallway, on its table,
Lay the family's great Bible.

In the dark, by lamplight stirred,
The Void grew pregnant with the Word.

In black ink they wrote it down.
The other ink was turning brown.

From the woods there came a cry—
A hoot owl asking who, not why.

The men sat silent on the porch,
Each lighted pipe a friendly torch

Against the unknown and the known.
But the child knew himself alone.

June 13, 1933

The morning sun rose up and stuck.
Sunflower strove with hollyhock.

I ran the worn path past the sty.
Nothing was hidden from God's eye.

The barn door creaked. I walked among
Chaff and wrinkled cakes of dung.

In the dim light I read the dates
On the dusty license plates

Nailed to the wall as souvenirs.
I breathed the dust in of the years.

I circled the abandoned Ford
Before I tried the running board.

At the wheel I felt the heat
Press upwards through the springless seat.

And when I touched the silent horn,
Small mice scattered through the corn.

June 14, 1933

I remember the soprano
Fanning herself at the piano,

And the preacher looming large
Above me in his dark blue serge.

My shoes brought in a smell of clay
To mingle with the faint sachet

Of flowers sweating in their vases.
A stranger showed us to our places.

The stiff fan stirred in mother's hand.
Air moved, but only when she fanned.

I wondered how could all her grief
Be squeezed into one small handkerchief.

There was a buzzing on the sill.
It stopped, and everything was still.

We bowed our heads, we closed our eyes
To the mercy of the flies.

"First Death" developed consciously, so far as the development was conscious, out of no more than a feeling many poets
must have conditioned themselves to respond to—the generalized desire simply to be writing a poem, any poem.* Having
been sick for some months, I had not been writing and was,
perhaps, beginning to feel guilty. A first worksheet shows that
I was typing out tetrameter couplets about nothing in particular. Since it is not my usual practice to *type* a first draft, I
suspect that I was merely practicing, trying to warm up, not
feeling altogether responsible for what my fingers might find
to say. Ultimately, about halfway down the first page, I typed
a couplet or two *about* something, about something specific
and real: raindrops caught in a spiderweb on a back porch. I
knew which porch that was—my grandparents' porch, on a
farm near Tifton, Georgia, some time in the early thirties.
(The detail was not to survive in the poem.) I rationalized the
process by supposing that, while my conscious mind was attending to details of rhyming and metering these couplets
about nothing, my unconscious had been freed to rove and
dive until it came up with a fragment of memory, entangled

---

*To a questionnaire sent out by Alberta Turner, who was editing a
book eventually to be published under the title *Fifty Contemporary
Poets* (New York: David McKay, 1977), I wrote this response. Most of
the points touched on and even the order in which they come up
were determined by the questionnaire itself.

with associations rich, for me, in feeling and significance. Why I was writing couplets at all I cannot remember. I had never published a poem in such couplets; indeed, I had not tried rhyme for years (except in a libretto that year for which the composer had requested rhyme), and I had never rejoiced in rhyming, being less than adept at it. I do recall feeling then that most poets were tending to write more and more sloppily and that some attention to the strictest formal etiquette might check that inclination insofar as I shared it. Nor did I wish simply to repeat myself, to write on and on of the themes and in the manners of *Departures*, the book I had recently completed. I would try to be new, at least for myself, by returning to the old—old form, old subject.

It is rare for a poem of mine to go through an orderly succession of drafts, versions which begin at the beginning and go right through to the end. The four or five drafts usually required in such cases are quickly done, and with pleasure. A different pleasure comes from the kind of work this poem involved, the pleasure resulting from care and labor, as in making something with tools in a manual training class or putting up a house of cards. Each line and, in this poem, each couplet had, it seemed, to be shaped into something close to its final form, or at least made to fill up its imagined place with more or less the right meaning, before I was ready to continue. Although there are no drafts except for very late ones, I can count thirty-four worksheets. Unhappily, long periods elapsed between intervals of work. If I started the poem some time in the summer of 1973, as I believe I did, and made substantial progress on it then, getting through much of the first two sections, I did not resume serious work on it till June, 1975. I was not sure how long the poem would or should be—couplets have a way of running on and on—but I did see it early as falling into parts (if not pieces), and once I had more than enough for the first two sections down on paper, it seemed that one last section, something conclusive, should suffice. What—I must have asked myself, on coming back to it—what more conclusive than the funeral itself? (The first funeral I had ever attended.) In this sense the poem expanded, grew, was added on to. But in other ways it just as clearly shrank, the first section from twenty or more lines to an exact sixteen, and similarly throughout. And if I had vaguely imagined a poem that might re-create the Georgia summers I had passed as a child—a part of my own lesser *Prelude*, so to speak—a poem of no fewer, surely, than two hundred lines; if, indeed, I must have written that many lines for it (though I do not wish to count the worksheets to verify the number), it nevertheless ended as a mere forty-eight, not a documentary of all that those Georgia summers had been, but an edited cinema of three days remembered from one summer only.

In the nature of the case, the structure, this once, did not much change, except for the fixing of the exact number of lines for each section. The theme changed only in being narrowed down and focused on my grandmother's death and my reactions as a child to that shaking, though common, experience. The tone, unfortunately, did undergo some modification. I had wanted from the first something childlike, folklike, near-primitive, feeling the couplet to be a fit vehicle for such a tone, and that tone to be in keeping with both the subject and, as might be remarked of a fiction or memoir, the child's point of view. The first two lines, I felt, set the tone I wanted to maintain. But I could not maintain it, despite effort. In what follows there is a growing self-consciousness, perhaps some reminiscence even of the handling of this particular verse line from Milton's great pair of poems, but I hope not so much as to spoil completely the innocence from which it started. The first two lines of the poem, then, are the unchanged lines, the model lines. Only slightly changed were the "witty" line about the Void, the lines about the hoot owl, and the final couplets of the first and last sections. Everything in the second section was considerably revised; signs of the trouble which that part gave me still seem visible. Most of the revisions seem to have been made for the sake of coherence—narrative, stylistic, and especially tonal.

The meters require little explanation and, in my view, no defense. The tetrameter couplet is a more flexible instrument than generally acknowledged, and the line itself may crop up anywhere from ballads to Milton. Its particular adaptation here is the one which allows you, depending on whether you regard the line as iambic or trochaic, to drop or to add a first syllable; in other words, the first foot is free. In "L'Allegro" and "Il Penseroso" this slight admixture of freedom opens the line to grace, beauty, and delight, and in this respect suggests the attractive waywardness with which the line is treated in certain ballads. Wishing to keep the tone casual and un-sophisticated, in tension with the apparent severity of the couplet, I was happy to find a handful of inexact rhymes. The metaphor, what there may be of it, is conventional or so simple as to escape notice. It seems to have become virtually a principle with me—in practice if not yet in theory—to use literal details so that they imply metaphor. Summer heat is equivalent to intense misery: temperature becomes meta-phor. When the child in the poem touches the dead horn of the old Ford and the mice scatter, the paradox of creatures responding to silence as if it were a sudden frightening noise is, I propose, metaphorical, an attempt to render the child's projection of his own terror onto his surroundings. As for language, anything that is not simple, not obviously rooted in the child's sensibility, is most likely to be traced to the op-pressive influence of the religion which afflicted that sen-sibility (as in lines 8 and 20). Against custom, including my own, I was willing to admit here and there certain old-fash-ioned "poetic" devices, such as inversion ("by lamplight stir-red"), easy enough otherwise to get around, on the grounds that they reinforced the tone I was after. I was trying to write a poem, not an exemplary text on how poetry ought to be written now or in the future.

The order of the poem is chronological, a narrative with a beginning, middle, and end, and with no more ellipsis than common in narrative, yet selective rather than accumulative, more like a short story than a novel. I wanted a big ending, quietly done. The boy in the poem is myself, but myself at seven, which gives me the illusion of distance I prefer to work with. I had, as usual, no particular audience in mind, but readers certainly, nameless readers. And for once, this was a poem I would have been glad to have my mother read, but she died before I finished it.

The outline of the poem is easy enough to paraphrase, and paraphrases that do not wallow in prolixity are of outlines only. Paraphrase: (1) A boy sees his grandmother die and is terrified by the mysteries and customs surrounding the death, feeling himself alone in a hostile world. (2) He hides himself away from others and attempts to know the past, to master it and escape from the present through an act of make-believe. (3) At the funeral he feels oppressed by the heat, the rituals, and the inefficacy of religious consolation. Such a paraphrase necessarily leaves out what I trust may seem the magical reality which comes about through the more detailed rendering and more substantial ordering required by the poem, though some of what is lost might be restored by expanding the prose commentary. (With a "creative" critic something might even be added.) What would be lost forever if only the prose commentary survived would be the pleasure (if any) of the meters and rhymes themselves and whatever effects of coherence, compression, and point their binding force had led to (or not prevented), all of which ought to have helped *fix* the poem, as the right solution fixes the snapshot. The reader would have lost the chance to experience the event for himself. I would have lost my own pleasure in having put the poem together in this way, in having made something, this.

The poem is not at all obscure, I think, and should give no one trouble on that score. How good or bad the poem may be is another question, one I cannot properly answer. I do like it. I like it because it records something otherwise lost.

(1975)

Meters and Memory

The mnemonic value of meters seems always to have been recognized. There are, to begin with, the weather saws, counting spells, and the like, which one does more or less get by heart in childhood. But any ornament, however trivial and even meaningless, probably assists the recollection to some degree, if by ornament we mean a device of sound or structure not required by the plain sense of a passage. Repetition obviously functions in this way—anaphora, refrains, even the sort of repetition which involves nothing more than an approximate equivalence of length, as in Pound's Sapphic fragment:

> Spring ....
> Too long ......
> Gongula.......

Likewise with such structural features as parallel parts or syllogistic order, whether in verse or prose. For that matter, fine and exact phrasing alone enables the memory to take hold about as well as anything. A friend of mine, at parties, preferred to recite prose rather than verse, usually, as I recall, the opening paragraph of *A Farewell to Arms*.

The purely mnemonic character of a passage, however, appears to contribute little to its esthetic power. Often enough rhymes are more effective mnemonically than meters, and occasionally other devices may prove to be. But the meters, where employed at all, are likely to be the groundwork underlying other figurations, hence basic, if not always dominant. Consider a couplet like "Red sky at morning, / Sailor take warning." Here the meters cooperate with the rhymes to fit the lines to one another, not only as lines of verse but as linked parts of a perception. It is no more than a slight exaggeration to claim that the couplet becomes fixed in memory by reason of this sense of fittedness. But few devices of sound are enough in themselves to ensure recall. Should, for example, the sky of the couplet be changed from red to blue, although neither rhyme nor meter would be affected, I cannot believe the couplet would survive. Survival in this case has something to do with aptness of observation, with use, that is, as well as cleverness or beauty. The kernel of lore provides a reason for keeping the jingle; the jingle preserves the lore in stable form.

Now all this is to consider memory, as is customary, from the viewpoint of an audience, as if a significant purpose of poetry were simply to put itself in the way of being memorized. For my part, when I am at work on a poem, the memory of an audience concerns me less than my own. While the meters and other assorted devices may ultimately make the lines easier for an audience to remember, they are offering meanwhile, like the stone of the sculptor, a certain resistance to the writer's efforts to call up his subject, which seems always to be involved, one way or another, with memory. (Hobbes somewhere calls imagination the same thing as memory.) In any case, memory is going to keep whatever it chooses to keep not just because it has been made easy and agreeable to remember but because it comes to be recognized as worth the trouble of keeping, and first of all by the poet. The audience will find it possible to commit to memory only what the poet first recalls for himself. Anything can be memorized, including numbers, but numbers that refer to something beyond themselves, as to the combination of a safe, are the easier to keep in mind for that reason. Something other than themselves may likewise be hidden in the meters, and an aptness to be committed to memory might almost be taken as a sign of this other presence. Pattern is not enough. The trivial and insignificant pass beyond recall, no matter how patterned, discounting perhaps a double handful of songs and nonsense pieces,* where the pattern itself has somehow become a part of what is memorable. But such a result is exceptional. What happens in the more serious and ordinary case is that some recollection of a person, of an incident or a landscape, whatever we are willing to designate as subject, comes to seem worth preserving. The question for the poet is how to preserve it.

One motive for much if not all art (music is probably an exception) is to accomplish this—to keep memorable what deserves to be remembered. So much seems true at least from the perspective of the one who makes it. Nor should any resemblance to the more mechanical functions of camera and tape recorder prove embarrassing; like a literary text in the making, film and tape also permit editing, room enough for the artist. Let emotion be recollected, in tranquillity or turmoil, as luck and temperament would have it. And then what? Art lies still in the future. The emotion needs to be fixed, so that whatever has been temporarily recovered may become as nearly permanent as possible, allowing it to be called back again and again at pleasure. It is at this point that the various aids to memory, and meter most persistently, begin to serve memory beyond mnemonics. Such artifices are, let us say, the fixatives. Like the chemicals in the darkroom, they are useful in developing the negative. The audience is enabled to call back the poem, or pieces of it, the poet to call back the thing itself, the subject, all that was to become the poem.

The transcription of experience represented by the meters ought not to be confused with the experience itself. At best the meters can perform no more than a reenactment, as on some stage of the mind. This being so, to object to the meters as unnatural because unrealistic is to miss the point. Like the odd mustaches and baggy pants of the old comedians, they put us on notice that we are at a certain distance from the

---

*Nonsense may be the condition, in any case, to which devices of sound in themselves aspire.

normal rules and expectations of life. The effect has been variously called a distancing or a framing. Wordsworth described it as serving "to divest language, in a certain degree, of its reality, and thus to throw a sort of half-consciousness of unsubstantial existence over the whole composition." The meters signify this much at least, that we are at that remove from life which traditionally we have called art.

Their very presence seems to testify to some degree of plan, purpose, and meaning. The meters seem always faintly teleological by implication, even in company with an anti-teleological argument, as the case may be. They are proof of the hand and ear of a maker (uncapitalized), even in a poetry which otherwise effaces the self. They seem to propose that an emotion, however uncontrollable it may have appeared originally, was not, in fact, unmanageable. "I don't know why I am crying" becomes "Tears, idle tears, I know not what they mean." The difference seems important to me. The poetic line comes to constitute a sort of paraphrase of the raw feeling, which will only get broken back down close to its original state in some future critic's reparaphrase. The writer in meters, I insist, may feel as deeply as the non-metrical writer, and the choice whether or not to use meters is as likely to be dictated by literary fashion as by depth of feeling or sincerity. Nevertheless, they have become a conventional sign for at least the desire for some outward control; though their use cannot be interpreted as any guarantee of inner control, the very act of writing at all does usually imply an attempt to master the subject well enough to understand it, and the meters reinforce the impression that such an attempt is being made and perhaps succeeding. Even so, the technology of verse does not of itself affirm a philosophy, despite arguments to the contrary. Certain recent critics have argued that even syntax is now "bogus," since the modern world contains no such order as that implied in an ordinary sentence, much less a metrical one. But the imitation theory underlying this argument seems naive and unhistorical to me, for it was never the obligation of words or of word-order to imitate conditions so reflexively. Syntax deals, after all, primarily with word-order, not world-order, and even the meters, or so it seems to me, can imitate only by convention.

Let me take a simple case. Yvor Winters once offered his line, "The slow cry of a bird," as an example of metrical imitation, not strictly of a birdcall itself but of "the slowness of the cry." The convention would seem to be that two or more strong syllables in succession carry associations of slowness and heaviness, while two or more weak syllables in succession carry contrary associations of rapidity and lightness: melancholy on the one hand, playfulness on the other. But the displacement of a stress from *of* to *cry* in the Winters line, bringing two stresses together, fails to slow the line down, as I hear it. Substitute for this "The *quick* cry of a bird," and the two weak syllables following *cry* can be said to do as much to speed the line up, or as little. But whether the cry is to sound quick or slow, the metrical situation itself remains, practically speaking, identical. If any question of interpretation arises from the reversed foot, the meaning of the reversal must depend on the denotation of the adjective rather than on the particular arrangement of syllables and stresses, for denotation overrides any implication of the meters apart from it. Though apparently agreed on by generations of poets, the minor convention on which Winters was depending is hardly observed any longer except in criticism or occasionally the classroom. Nor was it, for that matter, observed by Milton in his great melancholy-playful pair, "Il Penseroso" and "L'Allegro," or if observed, then only to be consciously played against. Composers of music for the movies learned early that direct imitation of a visual image through sound was best restricted to comic effects (pizzicati, trombone glissandi, staccato bassoons). Pushed far enough, and that is not very far at all, the results of metrical imitations can seem similarly cartoonlike:

> I sank to the pillow, and Joris, and he;
> I slumbered, Dirck slumbered, we slumbered all three.

In any case, simple imitation by means of rhythm would seem to be more plausible in free verse, with its greater flexibility, and most workable in prose, which is allowed any and every arrangement of syllables. The point seems obvious and incontrovertible to me, though never brought up in quite this way, I think. Wordsworth ascribes to the meters a different and greater power, finding in them a "great efficacy in tempering and restraining the passion by an intertexture of ordinary feeling," and, he goes on to add, "of feeling not strictly and necessarily connected with the passion." The meters move along in their own domain, scarcely intersecting the domain of meaning, except in some illusory fashion or by virtue of conventions nearly private. The responsibility they bear to the sense, comic writing aside, is mostly not to interfere. By so effacing themselves they will have accomplished all that they must accomplish in relation to the sense. Speech they can and do imitate, from a little distance, but rarely by quoting, that is to say, by attempting to become speech. Song they perhaps are or can become, their natural inclination; no question in that of imitating anything outside their own nature.

Whether their nature really embodies an imitation of natural processes may be arguable. But I do not think the meters can be, in any such sense, organic. A recognition of this, conscious or not, has been reason enough for their rejection by contemporary organicists, poets and critics both. The meters seem more to resemble the hammer-work of carpenters putting together a building, say, than waves coming in to shore or the parade of seasons. We do inhale and exhale more or less rhythmically, as long as we stay healthy; our hearts do beat without much skipping, for years on end. Breath and heart are the least remote of these similitudes, but any connection between them and the more or less regular alternation of weak and strong syllables in verse seems doubtful to me and, valid or not, need carry no particular prestige. In urban life, far from the Lake Country of 1800, are to be found analogies as appropriate as any from nature, if no more convincing. Signals timed to regulate the flow of traffic not only seem analogous but at times remarkably beautiful, as on a nearly deserted stretch of Ninth Avenue in New York City at three

A.M., especially in a mild drizzle. If the meters do represent or imitate anything in general, it may be nothing more (or less) than some psychological compulsion, a sort of counting on the fingers or stepping on cracks, magic to keep an unpredictable world under control.

Where the meters are supposed to possess anything of an imitative character, the implicit purpose must be to bring the poetic text closer to its source in reality or nature by making it more "like" the thing it imitates. Such an illusion may be enhanced if the poet's conviction is strong enough to persuade an audience to share his faith, but such conversions are more likely to be accomplished through cricitism than through poetry. The twin illusions of control and understanding seem more valuable to me than this illusion of the real, since it is through them, I suspect, that the meters are more firmly connected to memory. To remember an event is almost to begin to control it, as well as to approach an understanding of it; incapable of recurring now, it is only to be contemplated rather than acted on or reacted to. Any sacrifice of immediate reality is compensated for by these new perspectives. The terror or beauty or, for that matter, the plain ordinariness of the original event, being transformed, is fixed and thereby made more tolerable. That the event can recur only in its new context, the context of art, shears it of some risks, the chief of which may anyhow have been its transitory character.

If for an audience the meters function in part to call back the words of the poem, so for the poet they may help to call the words forth, at the same time casting over them the illusion of a necessary or at least not inappropriate fitness and order. There is a kind of accrediting in the process, a warrant that things are being remembered right and set down right, so long as the meters go on working. In this way the meters serve as a neutral and impersonal check on self-indulgence and whimsy; a subjective event gets made over into something more like an object. It becomes accessible to memory, repeatedly accessible, because it exists finally in a form that can be perused at leisure, like a snapshot in an album. Memory itself tends to act not without craft, but selectively, adding here to restore a gap, omitting the incongruous there, rearranging and shifting the emphasis, striving, consciously or not, to make some sense and point out of what in experience may have seemed to lack either. That other presence of which I spoke earlier—the charge of feeling, let us say, which attaches perhaps inexplicably to the subject, what the psychologist might call its *affect*—is not much subject to vicissitudes and manipulations of this sort, except for a natural enough diminution. It remains, but more than likely beneath the surface.

The meters are worth speculating about because they are so specific to the medium, if not altogether essential. Without them nothing may, on occasion, be lost; with them, on occasion, something may be gained, though whatever that is probably has little or nothing to do with sense or ostensible subject. This, in fact, appears to be the sticking point, that in themselves the meters signify so little. It seems a mistake for a rationalist defender of the meters to insist on too much meaningfulness. Let us concede that the effects of the meters are mysterious, from moment to moment imprecise, often enough uncertain or ambiguous. Like Coleridge's incense or wine, however, their presence may "act powerfully, though themselves unnoticed." To which he adds an interesting comparison to yeast—"worthless," as he says, "or disagreeable by itself, but giving vivacity and spirit to the liquor" in right combination. Meters do accompany the sense, like a kind of percussion only, mostly noise. Over and above syntax, they bind the individual words together, and the larger structural parts as well, over and above whatever appearance of logic survives in the argument; as a result, the words and parts seem to cohere, more perhaps than in plain fact may be the case. How they assist the recollection is by fixing it in permanent, or would-be permanent, form. This, for the poet, may be the large and rather sentimental purpose which gives force to all their various combining and intersecting functions.

(1975)

The Free-Verse Line in Stevens

Stevens is one of the very few masters of the traditional meters to have written free verse of a comparable power. Indeed, the two types of free-verse line Stevens favored—one short, one long—seem turned out with such easy skill, and the longer of the two with such loquacious facility, that critical attention to the verse itself tends to slip. Unlike some of his great contemporaries, Stevens never volunteered anything approaching a theory of versification as a guide to his own practice, and even the willing reader may fail to register what is going on prosodically. Hundreds and hundreds of pages of Stevens criticism are testimony to this sort of slippage. Aside from certain observations by J. V. Cunningham and Harvey Gross, the scanty prosodical commentary I have come across tends to exhaust itself in vague or baffled praise. This vacuum implies perhaps that the ideas of Stevens are more interesting than his verse or that what might be said of the verse is too obvious to be worth going into detail about. But Stevens' versification is a fascinating case, encompassing as it does both the traditional and the experimental. If he founded no schools and coined no prosodical terms, activities which tend to get the poet's own practice noticed, his versification is nevertheless thoroughly in the modern spirit; and some attempt to describe it with reasonable exactness and proper attention to detail, particularly in regard to his free verse, is overdue. Such an attempt necessarily involves a fair amount of technical discussion, and readers who believe technique has nothing to do with poetry should read no further.

Stevens' earliest free verse, like that of most of his contemporaries, was written in short lines. Such a line has been called the Imagist line. Stevens' version of it appeared within a year or two after Imagism had crossed the Atlantic, it is true, and this would be a historically convenient name for it, but it is also misleading, for in the Imagist anthologies the great majority of the lines prove to be longer than the line Stevens was using and only rarely as cleanly organized. Stevens' line is shaped syntactically; that, is, it stops at the end of a phrase or clause and does not break across the phrase or contrary to it. J. V. Cunningham has called it, condescendingly, a kind of "parsing" meter, since the syntactical parts of the sentence are, as it were, visually diagrammed by the line divisions. The point of the line divisions, however, seems to be not merely to follow the grammarian's parsing but to suggest a principle of order a little aside from grammar, implying a conscious and deliberate ordering of the phrases into units having a recognizable rhythmical as well as syntactical identity. The sense of the line becomes in itself a shaping force, a partial guide to the composition of the phrases and to their linkage. "Disillusionment of Ten O'clock," almost the earliest example, is also probably the most familiar.

> The houses are haunted
> By white night-gowns.
> None are green,
> Or purple with green rings,
> Or green with yellow rings,
> Or yellow with blue rings.
> None of them are strange,
> With socks of lace
> And beaded ceintures.
> People are not going
> To dream of baboons and periwinkles.
> Only, here and there, an old sailor,
> Drunk and asleep in his boots,

Catches tigers
In red weather.

If what may be called the Cunningham principle were the only guide, then lines 8 and 9 could with equal reason be printed as one line.

With socks of lace and beaded ceintures.

Further, lines 10 and 11 might be divided, with somewhat more reason, after *dream* instead of after *going*.

People are not going to dream
Of baboons and periwinkles.

In either case, the grammatical principle would continue to be upheld. Yet though the grammatical "rule" does have a certain use, it is neither exact nor sufficient. What it amounts to fundamentally is that the lines are never divided across the phrase, not, for instance, in the way Williams, about the same time, might have enjoyed arranging them:

Or purple with green
rings, or green with
yellow rings, or
yellow with blue rings. None . . .

But what further principle of order is present, if any? Only perhaps that a great preponderance of the lines will be so composed as to come out to about the same length as one another, in both look and sound, though the visual likeness is almost certainly of less moment than the aural. John Hollander, in another connection, offers the opinion that this type of line can be described as being about 25-em wide. Such a description emphasizes the visual rather than the aural, an emphasis quite reasonable with a good deal of verse that looks like this on the page. But it is the sound of poetry which remains primary, even in an age of visual experiment, and in any case a description in terms of measure by ruler or the spaces of a typesetter will not do for Stevens. There is more here than meets the eye, so to speak, and the presence of other determining features than the visual is one reason his verse can seem so rich and resonant, even when the ideas are relatively trivial or repetitive.

Attempting to measure the sound is more rewarding. The lines of "Disillusionment of Ten O'clock" are pretty obviously organized upon some sort of accentual basis, though the basis is just as obviously a somewhat flexible one. It is not that each line *must* contain two accents but that each line *may* and probably will do so. With any normal pronunciation and inflection and with any commonsense understanding of the troublesome word *accent*, most of the lines do have two accents. One line has three accents for certain, and several others appear to have two *or* three, depending a little on the way they are interpreted; two lines probably stretch out to four accents and one perhaps to as many as five. Exact agreement on these points is not very important. What matters is to recognize that the basic line contains a certain number of accents from which departures will occur; and this fact seems plain enough to be regarded as a clear organizing principle. It might not be pretty, but a mathematician would find it easy enough to devise a formula such as "2 accents plus or minus 1 (or more)" to describe this line in action. Each line is a kind of "variable foot," if Williams' term may be resurrected and put back into service, though not precisely in the Williams sense. I do not mean to suggest that Stevens formulated his idea of the line in just such a way and was constantly thinking about it during the act of composition. The poet's sense of the rhythm of the line was no doubt less mathematical in spirit; but that some such sense, however defined, did exist and was held in the mind of the poet while he wrote seems probable, to judge from the consequences in poem after poem. The point is that we can describe it, at least loosely; not that the poet did so, for most poets are not theoreticians.

Other features involving the metrical organization of the line appear from time to time, if not as decisively. Stevens likes the grammatical parallelism which has long been recognized as a means of organizing free verse, although it is more familiar in the long, rhetorical lines of the Psalms or of Whitman. Consider the color passage in "Disillusionment of Ten O'clock":

> Or purple with green rings,
> Or green with yellow rings,
> Or yellow with blue rings.

Here is a demonstration—on the poet's part a veritable exhibition—of the most fascinating aspect of parallelism in versification, namely, that units of a different length and type may be considered the same in the metrical "count." This recognition points to one of the basic pulls or tensions in free verse—in all verse, really—a tension between the competing claims of unity on the one hand and variety on the other. Williams, much later, demonstrates the same point, more jaggedly and professorially:

> back and
> forth and back and forth
> and back and forth

The longest line in "Disillusionment of Ten O'clock" is of special interest. It contains three or four or perhaps even five accents and is thus a departure from the norm.

> Only, here and there, an old sailor

But if we imagine the line as dividing after *there*, it looks like a line made up of two ordinary lines joined together—a double line, so to speak. The first half-line has two or three accents; the second half-line contains the standard two. The reason for not dividing this "double line" in the customary and predictable place may be just that the first half—"Only, here and there"—includes no matter of substance of consequence, no noun or verb, only the syntactical connecting phrase necessary to introduce the old sailor. If this inference is plausible, still another principle affecting the organization of the verse into lines, though not strictly a metrical one, may be glimpsed. Simply put, it would go something like this: each line as printed will contain matter of more than grammatical interest. (Incidentally, this was by no means a universal principle for the short-line free verse of this early experimental period, certainly not for Williams, who was willing to offer as complete lines mere prepositions like *at* or *of* or adverbs like *also* and *perhaps*. But in Stevens' free verse of the period no lines of this type can be found, no lines in violation of this apparent principle.)

It may well be some such consideration which helps to keep the short lines of this type of free verse packed and loaded with interest. If the lines seem relatively fast-paced, characterized by that very speed Williams claimed for American speech, it may be because they seem to contain a good deal in relation to length; much passes rapidly before eye and ear. In Stevens such lines seem active and lively in themselves, frequently fanciful, even beyond what the poet's own temperament brings of that spirit to them. They become rich in particulars, bristling with nouns and verbs, incapable, it would seem, of becoming discursive and philosophical, as Stevens in his longer lines does seem incorrigibly tempted to become.

If this short free-verse line were found in only one of Stevens' poems, metrical generalizations about it would be properly suspect. But a number of his contemporaries were also working with a line resembling it, and we can count about two dozen of Stevens' own poems based upon it, most of them in *Harmonium*, if we include, as seems reasonable, several poems based on a slightly longer line of three accents.

> Swiftly in the nights,
> In the porches of Key West,
> Behind the bougainvilleas,
> After the guitar is asleep,
> Lasciviously as the wind,
> You come tormenting,
> Insatiable . . .

On a few occasions Stevens wrote a stricter accentual verse, from which the more flexible line of "Disillusionment of Ten O'clock" or "O Florida, Venereal Soil" can be easily enough distinguished. The accentual line he prefers is longer, curiously of a middle length between the short "Disillusionment" line and the traditional pentameter of "Sunday Morning," out of which so much of his later versification was to evolve. "The Man with the Blue Guitar," for example, has four accents to the line, with few exceptions. Among the scattering of true accentual poems, "The American Sublime" comes closest to resembling the early short-line free verse. Each of its lines has two accents, unvaryingly; a few might be read differently—this is always true—but no other reading is necessary, as it is in "Disillusionment of Ten O'clock."

> And the sublime comes down
> To the spirit itself,
>
> The spirit and space,
> The empty spirit
> In vacant space.
> What wine does one drink?
> What bread does one eat?

Such rigor sets it apart from the earlier examples.

Sometimes the line is neither the unvarying accentual line of "The American Sublime" nor the varying free-verse line of "Disillusionment of Ten O'clock" but something in between, as in "The Death of a Soldier."

> Life contracts and death is expected,
> As in a season of autumn.
> The soldier falls.
>
> He does not become a three-days personage,
> Imposing his separation,
> Calling for pomp.

Death is absolute and without memorial,
As in a season of autumn,
When the wind stops,

When the wind stops and, over the heavens,
The clouds go, nevertheless,
In their direction.

It is convenient and reasonable to regard the prosody of this poem as accentual, but here the lines vary in length according to the pattern of the stanza. The first line of each stanza may be read with four accents, the second with three, and the third with two. All of this can be done quite naturally and without straining what may be thought of as the prose rhythm of the passage, and I believe it is generally better with Stevens, as it may not be with less skillful and artful poets, to read his meters as "regularly" as possible, to read, that is, with attention to the norm first and only then to whatever departures or variations there may be. As long as the lines remain gathered together into the predictable and recurring order dictated by the three-line stanza, the pattern allows the accentual meters to be heard and understood. Echoes of the old pentameters which were presumably the ancestors of these lines may be caught, but not very lingeringly. Those lines with three and two accents in succession—that is, the second and third lines of each stanza—never quite recombine into pentameters, not decisively, at any rate; nor are the lines with four accents, bound by the stanza as they are, permitted to lengthen out to the rather flabby pentameters they might have been taken for in a different setting.

He does nót becóme a thrée-days pérsonage

In a poem like *Notes toward a Supreme Fiction* the different context would lead the reader to construe such a line as a fairly typical loosened pentameter, with a weak verse-accent on the last syllable.

But not here: the stanza pattern argues against it, and context is always a factor in reading meters right. On the other hand, had the lines been distributed at random instead of being arranged into stanzas, the result would have been virtually indistinguishable from the type of free verse we have been trying to describe.

Still another kind of verse resembles this, for which we may borrow, for the sake of historical convenience, the old term, *vers libre*. Perhaps Eliot was right to claim, as he did about the time Stevens was writing these poems, that since it was to be defined only by negatives, by the absence of "pattern," "rhyme," and "metre," *vers libre* simply did not exist. Nevertheless the term has a limited usefulness, if we keep in mind the type of verse a number of French poets were writing in the second half of the nineteenth century, Laforgue, for one, whose poems Stevens knew. It was to describe their verse that the term *vers libre* had been invented, and it did indeed include some rhyme, at apparently haphazard intervals. The lines frequently varied in length and were not arranged into the strict stanza patterns of a poem like "The Death of a Soldier." The second section of "Peter Quince at the Clavier" is the best-known passage in Stevens written more or less to such a plan.

> In the green water, clear and warm,
> Susanna lay.
> She searched
> The touch of springs,
> And found
> Concealed imaginings.
> She sighed,
> For so much melody.
>
> Upon the bank, she stood
> In the cool
> Of spent emotions.
> She felt, among the leaves,

The dew
Of old devotions.

She walked upon the grass,
Still quavering.
The winds were like her maids,
On timid feet,
Fetching her woven scarves,
Yet wavering.

A breath upon her hand
Muted the night.
She turned—
A cymbal crashed,
And roaring horns.

If this can be imagined stripped of its rhymes—an impossibility, really, since the rhymes so patently contribute to the very invention—what would be left might serve as a model for the line of "Disillusionment of Ten O'clock." The number of accents per line varies from one (quite frequent) to four (rare). Although a sort of hesitation pattern may be observed in the alternation of slightly longer with slightly shorter lines, almost as in a dance step, nowhere does the variety in line length fall into a regular stanza pattern. It is true that the meters are iambic, with scarcely an exception, but the overall design remains "free." There is in fact more variety in line length than in the clearly free "Disillusionment of Ten O'clock." With a few adjustments—dropping the rhymes, varing the iambs a little—it is an easy passage from such *vers libre* to the free verse of "Disillusionment of Ten O'clock."

These are the boundaries of the short free-verse line in Stevens' own practice, but against the background of a broader historical context the line itself stands out even more clearly. It belongs, for one thing, roughly to the period of the First World War. The January, 1913, issue of the recently founded *Poetry* had led off with Vachel Lindsay's "General William Booth Enters Heaven," and included poems by such now-forgotten figures as Madison Cawein, Ernest Rhys, and Roscoe W. Brink; but what made the issue memorable was the small display of fireworks with which it ended—three poems by H.D., who, encouraged by Pound, signed herself "Imagiste." It remains a famous moment in modern literary history. The notes at the back of the issue characterized H.D.'s contributions, rightly, as "experiments in delicate and elusive cadences." One poem, called "Priapus," would soon become popular with anthologists under its eventual title, "Orchard."

> I saw the first pear
> as it fell—
> the honey-seeking, golden-banded,
> the yellow swarm
> was not more fleet than I,
> (spare us from loveliness)
> and I fell prostrate,
> crying:
> you have flayed us
> with your blossoms,
> spare us the beauty
> of fruit-trees.

A passage from still another poem in H.D.'s little group was to be quoted by Eliot a few years later with high approbation, alongside a passage from Matthew Arnold, as an example of the new verse. The effect of these first Imagist poems seems to have been that of a brightness streaking across the firmament, and it is impossible to suppose that Stevens and the well-to-do, dilettantish, mildly Bohemian, and very up-to-date circle of his literary acquaintances in Manhattan could have failed to take note. If most of the lines in the Imagist anthologies that followed were to prove longer than the free-verse line Stevens preferred at the time, they were longer than H.D.'s lines as well. If anything, Stevens' line was a version of the pure H.D. line. Pound himself, the leader and inventor of the movement, wrote almost nothing in so short a line. Yet somehow, in ways and for reasons which defy explanation, by the time "Disillusionment of Ten O'clock" was written (most likely in the summer of 1915*), this short line had already become available for use by a whole generation of young experimental poets in America, and their avant-garde journals for a time were filled with poems written in adaptations of it. Before 1915 was out, Stevens' acquaintance, Alfred Kreymborg, had brought out the first number of *Others*, probably the best of these journals, one which was to feature Stevens more than once during the months it survived. This short line was not the only experimental line going, but it was one of the most popular.

One of its accidental characteristics—though it is hard to be sure of the relation here between technique and content—was a high degree of fancifulness and exoticism. "Disillusionment of Ten O'clock" and Stevens' other early pieces using the line are in this respect quite typical, though less attenuated than many. A small anthology of passages, most of them drawn from *Others*, will show how much a product of the period the Stevens line was. These examples, representative as they are intended to be, do not seem to me totally negligible. They possess some style or stylishness, and a general air of liveliness often missing from the standard magazine verse of any given literary period. They seem almost to shine with an innocence and freshness available to lesser poets only perhaps at the beginning of these special literary moments.

> Blue undershirts,
> Upon a line,
> It is not necessary to say to you
> Anything about it—
> What they do,
> What they might do . . . blue undershirts.
>
> Orrick Johns (1915)

> The ice is glazing over,
> Torn lanterns flutter,
> On the leaves is snow.
>
> John Gould Fletcher (1915)

---

*See letter #195, dated July 25, 1915, in *Letters of Wallace Stevens*.

The white body of the evening
Is torn into scarlet,
Slashed and gouged and seared
Into crimson,
And hung ironically
With garlands of mist.
And the wind
Blowing over London from Flanders
Has a bitter taste.

Richard Aldington (1916)

Clear eyed flame
betrayer of earth
draw back from the sun!
Go in once more
to the wet grains, your secret.

Conrad Aiken (1916)

Fourteen queens:
Seven in gold,
Five in green,
And two
Are covered each
With an old-rose
Silk sari
Dotted with vermilion discs
And fringed with dusky gold.

Ferdinand Reyher (1916)

The wind in the pine trees
Is like the shuffling of waves
Upon the wooden side of a boat.

Amy Lowell (1917)

Trying to catch this line at the moment of its small, flashing glory in order to fix and examine its characteristics is a little like trying to deal with a specimen of bright insect in danger of extinction. Stevens himself was soon to let it slide from his repertory, and it seems to have survived through the thirties and afterwards as much by accident as through any consciousness of a tradition involving it. The Williams version of the short free-verse line was an exception, surviving, as it did, at least through early Creeley. But the Williams line was more nervous and erratic; it broke across sense and hurried always onward; it was self-consciously anti-literary and humble—working-class, it might be fair to say—and therefore, for better or worse, more serious and, at its worst, earnest, argufying, and preachy. The refreshingly light and charming line Stevens had used was to become rare through the generations that followed, almost unrecognized or unrecognizable. But not quite absent:

> Turned-over roots
> With bleached veins
> Twined like fine hair,
> Each clump in the shape of a pot.
> Theodore Roethke

> The nostrils of slow horses
> Breathe evenly,
> And the brown bees drag their high garlands,
> Heavily,
> Toward hives of snow.
> James Wright

> A cheekbone,
> A curved piece of brow,
> A pale eyelid,
> Float in the dark,
> And now I make out
> An eye, dark,
> Wormed with far-off, unaccountable lights.
> Galway Kinnell

The last line is reminiscent of the "double line" in Stevens, and like many such lines turns out to be an only slightly unusual pentameter.

> And still I lie here,
> bruised by rain, gored
> by the tiny horns
> of sprouting grass.
> Gregory Orr

For this to fit the model of the Stevens line more nearly, *gored* would have to be dropped down to the third line, but otherwise it is recognizably the same. It is as though over successive decades this old Stevens line, dating back to the First World War, could be glimpsed from time to time surfacing briefly, only to sink back again almost immediately into obscurity.

Yet the line might have its uses still. In practice it seemed especially well suited to journal-like jottings involving, often enough, exotic landscapes. If ever vaguely Oriental poems, modest in scope, with a relaxed air and a certain wit, should come into fashion, this is the line in which they might well be written.

Except for the historical authority of the term *free verse*, the line could be described as "loose accentuals," by analogy with what Frost called "loose iambics." Incidentally, Stevens himself wrote one poem in Frost's loose iambics, "Waving Adieu, Adieu, Adieu." Otherwise, even when stretching his own iambic pentameter line out almost to the breaking point, he approached loose iambics—a light, galloping meter—only briefly, intermittently, and apparently without intention, and "loose iambics" ought not to be confused with the "loose accentuals" of his short-line free verse.

A poet has his more solemn moments as well. If he has once fallen under the sway of a Harvard philosopher, as both Eliot and Stevens happened to do, he will, on the evidence, be drawn irresistibly toward that sort of wordy commerce with ideas which seems to require not only pages of illustrations, in Stevens' phrase, but longer lines as well. The short line clearly would not do for the development of ideas, which may be one of its virtues for the lyric, though not for the kind of poem Stevens had come by the end of *Harmonium* to be interested in. In the very narrowness of the short line there was simply no room for the occasional polysyllable, the obligatorily complex phrasing, and certainly not if the line, refusing to break across grammar and sense, was to retain its identity and autonomy, as it had done in Stevens' handling. Quite early it became apparent that Stevens would not remain content with the individual short poem written in this line, the sort of poem which in retrospect we can see resembles a single illustration of some larger point in the longer poems to come. Already, as in "Six Significant Landscapes" or "Thirteen Ways of Looking at a Blackbird," the instances and illustrations had begun to multiply.

There was no need for Stevens to go in search of a line that would fit his maturing and expanding purposes. The line was there already, and he had used it, beautifully, with a perfect early mastery rarely given to any poet; beyond that, the line itself reached back through the centuries, during which it had proved adaptable enough to serve for dramatic and narrative occasions as well as meditative.* This was the English heroic line, the unrhymed iambic pentameter of "Sunday Morning," "Le Monocle de Mon Oncle," and the rest of a brilliant handful in *Harmonium.* But during the course of Stevens' long career, the forty years from 1915 to 1955, this line as he used it underwent a series of changes which follow an eventually predictable but always interesting course. Beyond its interest in Stevens' own poetry its development stands as an example in the history of modern versification. Toward the end, Stevens evidently felt quite comfortable writing a long line that had become in essence "free," yet without ever quite losing touch with its source in the old heroic line, which more and more bends to his will without losing its shape.

It had been Eliot's opinion that "the most interesting verse" took a very simple form, like the iambic pentameter, and constantly withdrew from it, or took no form at all, and constantly approximated to a very simple one. With his short free-verse line, which did constantly approximate to a very simple form, Stevens had followed the second course. Now, with his iambic pentameter, he was to take the other course, constantly withdrawing from the simple form, treating it with ever increasing casualness—the easy condescension of the

---

*Stevens did not long remain much interested in the dramatic or the narrative; curiously, when he did try verse in drama, he employed his own short line.

master—until in the general loosening process both the iambic and the pentameter were to become nearly inaudible. Only the pattern, or in some lines the mere outline of a pattern, was left.

Pound, early in his career, working from the common iambic toward looser rhythms, took his descent in part from Browning, as Harvey Gross, among others, has observed, and Eliot from the minor Elizabethan and Jacobean dramatists, as he himself suggested; but the later Stevens, following along the same path of loosening the common iambic, seems to descend from no one so much as from the younger Stevens himself. All that he was to do later with this line is implicit in the blank-verse poems of *Harmonium.* The gradual evolution of the line can be seen as one more example of the classic pattern of the poet's development, in which the young poet first masters a type of traditional verse and then, maturing, treats its laws with more and more familiarity and confidence, leading to a degree of freedom. In Shakespeare's blank verse a similar progress or, depending on one's point of view, decline may be traced; his dramatic line started off as a strict line, with clearly placed and rather obvious accents, and ended slack, with accents less declamatory, more conversational. In Milton, *Paradise Lost* represents a more personal and theoretical treatment of the blank-verse line than *Comus*, an exploration of possibilities that was to culminate, for better or worse, in the choral experiments of *Samson Agonistes*. Likewise with Stevens, the fresh, untroubled blank verse of "Sunday Morning" gives way gradually to the looser blank verse of *Notes toward a Supreme Fiction* and, a little later, "Esthétique du Mal," only to end in the much loosened and stretched pentameters of "To an Old Philosopher in Rome," "St. Armorer's Church from the Outside," and "The World as Meditation." To include "Prologues to What Is Possible" would be to push the case about as far as it could be taken.

But before tracing the history of this line in detail, it is worth stopping to note briefly a quite different type of long line which Stevens dabbled in but did not pursue. Its very difference should help to define the particular type of loosened pentameter which was to prove so attractive to Stevens. This other long line appears to stem from prose, perhaps from French poetry in prose. The poems in question are early, "The Silver Plough-Boy" and "Indian River."

> The trade-wind jingles the rings in the nets around the
>   racks by the docks on Indian River.
> It is the same jingle of the water among the roots under the
>   banks of the palmettoes,
> It is the same jingle of the red-bird breasting the orange-
>   trees out of the cedars.
> Yet there is no spring in Florida, neither in boskage perdu,
>   nor on the nunnery beaches.

The accents in these lines, eight or nine probably, but indefinite as metrical accents, are hard to count because for the meters evidently they do not matter. Neither does the syllable count matter, as it would matter in the verses Marianne Moore was to turn to a few years afterward; and these modest experiments are hardly brassy and overwrought enough to qualify as the so-called polyphonic prose Amy Lowell was publishing at the time. What can be said about the lines is that they are quite long, all much the same length, however that length is to be measured, and prosy, relaxed, undefined.

By contrast Stevens' line based on the iambic pentameter has a distinct and recognizable sound. The accents can ordinarily be heard and counted; indeed, it is still "foot verse," which is to say that the syllables gathered about each verse accent, though varying to some degree, are distributed in a limited number of recurring and identifiable groupings. This was not true of the loose accentuals of "Disillusionment of Ten O'clock." For the purpose of definition it may be enough to say that Stevens' long line based on the iambic pentameter can be described as "free" when two conditions are met. One: when within a basically pentameter passage a few hexameters or tetrameters, rarely any line longer or shorter than these, are mingled randomly, yet without leading to metrical incoherence. Two: when as many non-iambic feet as iambic appear, as well as occasional lines or feet not easy to classify or interpret. Not often does Stevens allow his long line to venture this far from its source in blank verse, and then mostly toward the end of his career, but the tendencies of his blank verse did lead unmistakably for twenty-five years and more in this direction. Over the years the number of feet other than iambic increase; so too the number of lines other than pentameter. It is not enough to praise Stevens' versification, as critics conventionally do, for its "incomparable richness of rhythm and texture." The facts justify no such vagueness. The versification amounts to "a change in prosodic style," as Harvey Gross has said, a shift away from the firmness and resonance of blank verse to a relative freedom whose blank-verse rhythm "surges forward at times, then fades and dissolves into other cadences." This is the best description available of what characteristically happens to the long line in Stevens. Yet these "other cadences" are, strangely, hardly ever more than what Gross calls "anapestic stretching."

For what is remarkable and unexpected about Stevens' practice is that, within the generally loosening line, the foot itself is loosened almost exclusively in one way only: an anapest takes the place of the basic iamb. In the history of versification this is probably unprecedented. In Stevens the traditionally reversed foot, a trochee for an iamb, does occasionally appear, but far more common and indeed characteristic is his addition of a third syllable to the two syllables of the basic iamb—"anapestic stretching." Conventionally, extra syllables of this type are thought to lighten the movement of the line, but the effect of lightness is intermittent in Stevens' handling and surely no significant part of the metrical intention. At first it may seem surprising that through such simple means of variation the lines end up sounding as various as they do, so nearly verging on the irregular; later, after the tune has been caught and caught again, the means do at times seem too slender to avoid a certain monotony. A further variety comes, as it does in Milton, from moving the caesura to various points across the line, and in this Stevens is unquestionably skillful, though rather casual about it. In the long run, however, the mobility of the caesura is hardly enough to sustain long passages. With this much anapestic stretching, it may seem peculiar that more violence is not permitted the line, still more extraordinary departures sought and found. But with few exceptions no further testing of the line occurs. Compared to the metrical adventures of some of his contemporaries, Stevens' own experiments seem modest, but at the same time refreshingly clear and certain and, especially for short stretches, compelling and authoritative.

The stages in the development of this nearly "free" long line are progressive and can be charted. The initial and most traditional stage is that of "Sunday Morning" and most of the blank-verse poems in *Harmonium*. Here the line is classical, Elizabethan, more given to traditional means of gaining metrical variety, such as the reversed foot, than to the later multiplication of trisyllabic feet.

> There is not any haunt of prophecy,
> Nor any old chimera of the grave,
> Neither the golden underground, nor isle
> Melodious, where spirits gat them home,
> Nor visionary south, nor cloudy palm
> Remote on heaven's hill, that has endured
> As April's green endures; or will endure
> Like her remembrance of awakened birds,
> Or her desire for June and evening, tipped
> By the consummation of the swallow's wings.

The next stage—Stevens in mid-career—would include the versification of what some critics have considered his masterpiece, *Notes toward a Supreme Fiction*. The verse here, with its growing number of trisyllabic feet, has become more conversational, though hardly Frostian, altogether more relaxed, more circumlocutious and expansive, and certainly no longer Elizabethan.

> On a blue island in a sky-wide water
> The wild orange trees continued to bloom and to bear,
> Long after the planter's death. A few limes remained,

Where his house had fallen, three scraggy trees weighted
With garbled green. These were the planter's turquoise
And his orange blotches, these were his zero green,

A green baked greener in the greenest sun.

The final stage is well represented by "The World as Meditation," a poem in which, although both line-length and foot have become unstable, the blank-verse lineage is still apparent.

The trees had been mended, as an essential exercise
In an inhuman meditation, larger than her own.
No winds like dogs watched over her at night.

She wanted nothing he could not bring her by coming
    alone.
She wanted no fetchings. His arms would be her necklace
And her belt, the final fortune of their desire.

From about the midpoint of Stevens' career on, practically any trisyllabic substitution imaginable can be found. But in "Sunday Morning," the earliest blank-verse poem, there is only one trisyllabic foot that cannot be accounted for by elision, and even with it elision could be regarded as conventional, as in Renaissance practice.

By the consummation of the swallow's wings.

Nevertheless, this can be viewed as a historic moment, for out of this small seed the anapest was to become fruitful and multiply. The most common place to expect it is, as in the line from "Sunday Morning," the first foot:

The reverberating psalm, the right chorale

A forgetfulness of summer at the pole

But substitution in the second foot is not unusual in middle and late Stevens:

The soldier is poor without the poet's lines

The step to the bleaker depth of his descents

Of crimson and moods of Venezuelan green

Or in the third:

The mass of meaning becomes composed again

The truth depends on a walk around the lake

Matisse at Vence and a great deal more than that

Or in the fourth:

The wrinkled roses tinkle, the paper ones

A little thing to think of on Sunday walks

Occasionally a light but pleasant drag is felt when the extra syllable is heavier than usual:

For whom the good of April falls tenderly

And, finally, in the fifth position:

To naked men, to women naked as rain

And still the grossest iridescence of ocean

The commonplace became a rumpling of blazons

In Stevens' later verse all five feet in a pentameter are treated equally, as the examples indicate, with the result that his special anapest may show up freely at any place along the line.

The next and quite logical extension of this freedom is for several trisyllabic substitutions to appear together in the same line. Probably the earliest true instance of this phenomenon in Stevens comes from "The Comedian as the Letter C."

So much for that. The affectionate emigrant found

With the addition of this liberty, Stevens becomes less and less likely to write his pentameter line in the traditional way. He does not, for example, choose to write "Breakfast in Paris, music, madness, mud" as a classical pentameter but adds the Stevens touch, his personal trisyllabic fingering:

> Breakfast in Paris, music and madness and mud

A few more examples of multiple trisyllabic substitution, from two anapests to four a line, suggest the range.

> In the high imagination, triumphantly
> _____
> The west wind was the music, the motion, the force
> _____
> It was how he was free. It was how his freedom came
> _____
> Pipperoo, pippera, pipperum. The rest is rot
> _____
> An abysmal migration into a possible blue

Lines like this abound, as well as lines similar to them but in one way or another ambiguous. Trisyllabic substitution is the simplest and therefore probably the best way of accounting for an overwhelming majority of such lines; it seems in fact to be the very key to the late meters.

A few special effects involving trisyllabic substitution are worth singling out. One is what for convenience we might call "the Prufrock line."

> Let us go then, you and I,
> While the evening is spread out against the sky
> Like a patient etherized upon a table

Considered as foot verse, the first three syllables in each of these lines may be taken as either a falling rhythm or a rising rhythm: $/\check{}/$ or $\check{}\,\check{}/$. Both readings are simple and plausible, but the second reading is probably better, since it allows the second and third lines to be discerned as pentameters, which is surely their point of departure. Stevens is fond of the effect:

Like a body wholly body, fluttering

———

There would still remain the never-resting mind

———

With the broken statues standing on the shore

But Stevens uses also a special adaptation of this foot, rare in the work of others, in which the first syllable is light, the second possibly heavy, and the third surely heavy: ˘// or ˘ ˘/.

To sing júbilas át exáct, accústomed tímes.

In the light of Stevens' predilections, treating the first foot as an unusual version of the trisyllabic foot seems simpler than looking for some other explanation, as so astute an analyst as Harvey Gross does:

To síng júbilas at exáct, accústomed tímes.

A run of four consecutive unaccented syllables, as required by this scansion, is very rare and exists elsewhere chiefly in legend, I think, and "The Wreck of the Deutschland." But however described, this way of starting the line is not unusual in Stevens. It first shows up as early as "Le Monocle de Mon Oncle":

A blue pigeon it is, that circles the blue sky

He likes the effect so well that he tries it again almost at once:

A white pigeon it is, that flutters to the ground

Other examples:

A blue woman, linked and lacquered, at her window

> A dead shepherd brought tremendous chords from hell

> A thing final in itself and, therefore, good

> The sea shivered in transcendent change, rose up

> The sun aches and ails and then returns halloo

> The one moonlight in the simple-colored night

At other positions in the line it is rarer:

> All men endure. The great captain is the choice

So unusual a foot appearing so frequently in blank verse is unprecedented, so far as I know, outside Stevens' work; it becomes a small stroke in his signature. Something like it may be found perhaps in the meters of a poem like Shelley's "The Sensitive-Plant," which are basically a sort of anapestic tetrameter, but the kinship is remote:

> And each flower and herb on Earth's dark breast

> Like young lovers, whom youth and love makes dear

In Stevens' practice it is a step in the direction of turning the line loose, making it free.

A well-known metrical event, the "sprung" foot, produces an effect in passing somewhat like this. By a "sprung" foot I mean one from which a light syllable is dropped, with the result that two accents fall side by side in the line. Stevens very infrequently resorts to the sprung foot, which, whether consciously employed or not, has become more common in the work of other poets, especially of younger generations. In Stevens most of the places where the foot has apparently been sprung can be resolved into instances of the "blue pigeon" type. But there are exceptions:

> It was almost time for lunch. Pain is human

―――――

Wreathed round and round the round wreath of autumn

And perhaps:

Of nights full of the green stars of Ireland

There are, naturally enough, lines which fall less easily into categories. Almost unaccountable, they contribute to the reader's strong sense of increasing freedom or irregularity in Stevens' long line. One rhetorical device in particular tempts Stevens into inventing rhythms new to him and to the history of blank verse—the repetition of a word or a phrase, often in a parallel grammar. It is a device to which he seems much drawn. Occasionally it leads him to write a stretched out hexameter:

Universal delusions of universal grandeurs

―――――

Generations of shepherds to generations of sheep

Sometimes a parallel grammar in itself, without verbal repetition, produces a similarly stretched out line.

The sun shone and the dog barked and the baby slept

Even when the line is not lengthened, the feet may be combined in unusual ways:

Down-pouring, upspringing and inevitable

―――――

Without rain, there is the sadness of rain

―――――

The freshness of night has been fresh a long time

These last two lines are particularly notable. In them a rhythm of great metrical sophistication is crossed with the prose of common speech; both possibilities seem held in a mutually beneficial balance.

By such limited means and special adaptations Stevens eventually arrives at the point of composing a line free or so nearly free as to make little difference, yet with the skeleton of blank verse still faintly discernible in it:

A dumb sense possesses them in a kind of solemnity

From such a line it is only a stone's throw or perhaps a tongue's slip to this:

One thinks, where the houses of New England catch the
    first sun

This line represents the final stage in the loosening of Stevens' long line, and it comes very late. The poet did not live to explore it further, if indeed it can be stretched any further without losing all shape and identity.

This procrustean blank-verse line has proved to be one of the most prevalent of the century, even when not recognized or acknowledged for what historically it is. It has been part of the practice of verse for a long time now, and for some of the younger poets writing it the line may seem to exist independent of history, as if it had always been available. Even before Stevens, Eliot had found in the dramatists of Shakespeare's time a model for his own early departures from the standard iambic pentameter:

I that was near your heart was removed therefrom
To lose beauty in terror, terror in inquisition

Toward the end of his writing life his version of the line had slackened into this:

To explore the womb, or tomb, or dreams; all these are
    usual
Pastimes and drugs, and features of the press:
And always will be, some of them especially
When there is distress of nations and perplexity
Whether on the shores of Asia, or in the Edgware Road.

This passage, like many passages in Stevens, contains lines longer than the standard pentameter, together with several trisyllabic or otherwise stretched out feet, but the blank-verse line survives as a ghostly presence. Pound also tried the line, though it never became a favorite of his:

> A yellow stork for a charger, and all our seamen

Or in a satiric vein:

> The mauve and greenish souls of the little Millwins
> Were seen lying along the upper seats

Passages resembling these metrically from the work of later poets are not hard to find. Some stay close to the iambic base, while others range farther from it; but usually what Eliot had called "the ghost of some simple metre" apparently still lurks behind the arras.

> It is now she begins to sing—at first quite low
> Then loud, and at last with a jazzy madness—
> The song of her whistle screaming at curves,
> Of deafening tunnels, brakes, innumerable bolts.
> And always light, aerial, underneath
> Goes the elate meter of her wheels.
>> Stephen Spender

> Tired and unhappy, you think of houses
> Soft-carpeted and warm in the December evening
> While snow's white pieces fall past the window
>> Delmore Schwartz

> That speaks, in the Wild of things, delighting riddles
> To the soul that listens, trusting . . .
>> Poor senseless Life . . .
>> Randall Jarrell

> Always the silence, the gesture, the specks of birds
> suspended on invisible threads above the Site,
> or the smoke rising solemnly, pulled by threads
>> Elizabeth Bishop

The night is warm and clean and without wind.
The stone-white moon waits above the rooftops
and above the nearby river. Every street is still
                                        Mark Strand

Passages more regular than these could have been drawn
from the work of most of these poets, but trying to show the
line at that precarious point of balance between firmness and
collapse, where the tension between the drag of the past and
the pull of the future can be most vividly felt, seems more
characteristic and revealing.

Stevens' version of this line is only his own very special
adaptation of a line coming into general currency even as he
developed it. Its development in his work, however, follows a
straightforward and progressive course, and he uses it more
systematically and persistently than other poets seem to have
done. The Stevens line may therefore be seen as exemplary,
both historically and practically. It remains one of the two or
three most important verse lines of the modern period, and
Stevens is its most systematic master.

(1982)

On Purity of Style

And where a man may say that
Pindar many times praiseth
highly victories of small moment,
matters rather of sport than of
virtue . . . so indeed the chief
fault was in the time and custom
of the Greeks, who set those toys
at so high a price.

—Sir Philip Sidney

Between Walls

the back wings
of the

hospital where
nothing

will grow lie
cinders

in which shine
the broken

pieces of a green
bottle

This is a small, painterly poem by the doctor who had wanted
perhaps to be a painter, whom the Armory Show of 1913

greatly excited, whether or not he actually saw it, one of the early champions of the Cubists, a companion of artists. A painting in words and, like some of the new painting, it seems to occupy a shallow, severely delimited space, flat, one-dimensional. The objects are sparse, mostly drab.* They seem disposed on the page in part as a composition for the eye rather than the ear, yet rhythmically still, for the ear, by way of a syntactical arrangement requiring constant alertness. (The impression that this is an easy prose sentence is an illusion.) The climax comes about largely because the one touch of vivid color has been saved for the end—those broken pieces of green bottle—a final appeal to the visual sense. One of Williams' anthology pieces, it is so definitive an instance of the art of limited means that it seems still to mark off, fifty or so years later, one possible extreme of verbal expression. Doubtless the ground had been prepared by "In a Station of the Metro" and other Imagist pieces, but the first effect, two generations ago, can perhaps be imagined as mildly breathtaking, for those able to respond at all. That so much, esthetically speaking, could be claimed for so little!—the little gasp of astonishment remains a part of the intended effect, however matter-of-fact the delivery.

"Between Walls" is not of course a found object, not like Duchamp's pickax, praised by Williams, though it does come comfortably close. Newspaper clippings, transactions of the proceedings of historical societies, letters from friends: only perhaps items such as these could come closer to being truly found verbal objects, and it would be years yet before Williams was to paste such matter up into the large context of *Paterson*. Without some larger context into which it might be seen as fitting, this small early landscape suggests something like the art of the photograph. The artist, Williams, frequent visitor at Stieglitz' old gallery 291, intervenes only so far as to select what the eye of the camera is to record. The objects as they are caught remain totally static, though in some other poems be-

---

*Williams in the fifties: "We were writing poems from the dung-heap—the Ashcan School."

longing more or less to the same genre, the well-known cat poem among them, we would find movement. Here, however, the camera is a still camera. What moves is the eye of the beholder, down the page, led by the syntax, towards the visual climax: as the eye might trace the composition of photograph or painting. The shortness of the lines presumably is to ease, even to speed, this progress of the eye downwards, aided by the preponderance of unsyntactical line breaks. American, Williams thought it.

The complaint Sidney mentions is just such a complaint as might be lodged against much of Williams, that the victories he praises are of small moment; and the defense might well be, like Sidney's of Pindar, a cultural excuse. We Americans value our material objects, and Williams gives them back to us in words. Beyond that was the drive to purify the dialect of the tribe; and in the main American poetry was, when Williams started out, in need of some purification, as periodically it has been ever since, not taking purification to signify anything like genteel uplift. To purify "American" was no mean cultural motive. Yet there is more to be said, even of such small toys as Williams', to justify the price we set on them.

Happened upon though their objects seem to be, they have clearly been selected. The rhetorical stance may be to pretend that the selection is random, but in "Between Walls" it is not. The air of the casual is reassuring, but we are aware that the objects have been rescued from our habit of neglect by the noticing eye of an observer superior to ourselves. The eye finds not only the objects but a relation between them: it is at that instant that the shutter clicks. To fix these things and their relation in a language so transparent as Williams' remains here makes available to others the interest and importance locked away till now in the "found." And yet—and yet the act of choosing is a clue that points through, or beyond, the objects themselves to the one who chose, to the character of the perceiver and recorder, to *his* attitudes, *his* values. Williams was, from all accounts, a solid egotist. In other poems, early and late, he appears front-stage center, un-abashedly, the happy genius of his household and townfull of objects. Amazing that he should have managed in such poems as "Between the Walls" the illusion of having withheld, even withdrawn, himself; and more decisively than the enemy, Eliot, espouser of the very doctrine of self-effacement, ever managed the trick. Or so it may seem to us now.

In the face of such neglect as has surely been exaggerated—by Williams himself as well as by his recent biographer—he held confidently, even arrogantly, and certainly with good cause to his own path, which was for him the right track, while persuading himself and others that it was the only right track for everyone. In the face of such suffering as he saw, being a doctor, and of such ugliness, being a citizen of New Jersey, he remained, with understandable qualifications, an optimist, one who could go on for years finding a certain joy and beauty practically anywhere, almost by inadvertence, one who did often praise victories of small moment. This seems to me neither good nor bad in itself. It is simply how he was. But the point is that this attitude, far from being hidden in the bareness of the Imagist or Objectivist* poems, is in fact revealed by them. Stevens, the surfaces of whose poems are much more opulent, finds cause, as a rule, only for the stoic resolution of a determined pessimist confronting the American scene: "The empty spirit / In vacant space." His acquaintance Williams, even between walls, where "nothing will grow," among cinders, though it is in broken fragments, discovers a green that actually shines. This object on which he focuses, without being put through any of the usual rhetorical transformations of the verbal art, becomes, as placed, an image or emblem. And the glass reflects the man. It affirms, brightly.

The notes above were set down for a lecture in 1967, and I find myself now making a few changes to bring them up to date, none of much consequence. As I see the case now, there is one point these old notes seem to be driving at which never quite gets articulated but which counts a lot for me these days.

---

*"Between Walls" has been called both.

It seems crucial, in fact; and especially so perhaps in view of the present condition of American poetry. Far more than the *reality* of the scene, which I nonetheless highly prize, I would call attention now to the absolute purity of style achieved in this little masterpiece, and effortlessly achieved, rarely to be equalled even by Williams. Other poems by Williams—certainly poems by other poets—are much richer in what they encompass, their vision is deeper, the character of the poet stands as a more affecting human presence. Often enough the language is more brilliant. But this poem is perfectly said. Lean, streamlined: and there is nothing extra, no excrescence, no excess, no showing off; nor indeed any shortcoming whatever. We have what we see; we have it exactly. Art can aspire higher and no doubt, at times, should. But not always. I think of Wang Wei, the Chinese effect in general, here naturalized. I begin to understand how a critic like Winters can argue that the brief lyric may be greater than a complete tragedy, since the lyric can hope for perfection, an unflawed wholeness and unity. One of Williams' many admirers has written of "Between Walls" that since "there is no living thing in the poem—just a mockery of the color of growing plants— the feeling of the poem is . . . sterile and airless." But this opinion can only be the result of an absurd prejudice, probably got up out of some all too simple understanding of the organic and the natural. There is no mockery in this green: imitation, yes, and, one might even suggest, a certain pathos and bravery in the imitation. There is more to it than that, but there *is,* just glintingly, that. Meanwhile we do have also, thanking the muse of reality, pieces of a broken bottle, the real thing, as good as any green leaf here. Like Breughel, the poet saw it and with "grim / humor faithfully / recorded / it," confident that that was, if anything was, enough.

(1967–1983)

Bus Stop

Or, Fear and Loneliness on Potrero Hill

That fall and winter we were living in a rented house on Potrero Hill. From the back porch on the second story, where the living quarters were, you could look down into the neglected garden below or off across hills to the bay and the lights of Oakland. It was an exemplary view, but in a dark mood it could leave you feeling remote and isolated. We seemed to be perched insecurely on the top of an unfamiliar new world, teetering on the continent's very edge. Every evening I would walk our dog, Hugo, up and down the steep sidewalks, past the rows of narrow two-storied San Francisco houses, as the sun faded across their pale pastel fronts. High wooden fences surrounded some of them, and through the palings you could see strange plants in tubs and the deep-hued blooms of exotic flowers.

Our nearest corner, the intersection of Kansas and 20th Streets, was a municipal bus stop. It seemed that often, just as we were setting out on our walk, a bus would be stopped there, discharging passengers. At that hour they would be city workers coming home from their day in shop or office. There must have been an unusually long period of rain that year, two or three weeks of it, and I remember the passengers one after the other opening their great black umbrellas as they stepped down from the bus, which waited purring and quivering in the mist and drizzle of early evening. I sensed something symbolic in this, as if centuries hence it might be recalled as part of an ancient urban ritual whose meaning had been forgotten. And vividly there rose up before me a picture of the raised umbrellas which had represented the dead in the last scene of *Our Town,* called back now from the pages, years before, of *Life* magazine.

Sometimes, as we walked, the streetlights would wink on all at once, perfectly timed. Gradually more and more lights would be visible in the upper windows of the houses. From the playground you could see headlights moving along the Bayshore Highway just at the foot of the hill; or, from another bluff, the distant shunting in the Southern Pacific yards; all around, masked at times by fog, hung the various glows of the fanned-out districts of the city. It was beautiful. But the Potrero Hill of those days was like a lost village high in the Caucasus, with old Russian women peering doubtfully out from windows and doorways at passing strangers. All that fall and winter I felt like an exile, no part of the life around me. I knew none of the bus passengers alighting, no one in the lighted rooms above, certainly none of the wrinkled old women in their babushkas, who would yell and gesticulate sometimes at the quiet and well-mannered Hugo.

Such was the background from which "Bus Stop" gradually emerged. Other poems from that time share the same moods: "Poem to Be Read at 3 A.M." (with its own image of a burning light), "Memory of a Porch," "In the Greenroom," and "At a Rehearsal of *Uncle Vanya.*" (I was with a theater company that year, The Actor's Workshop.) The somewhat visionary "To the Hawks" came just after.

Connections between the life a writer lives and the work that comes out of that life seem much more important now than I once thought them, and in fact I would insist on their importance. Even so, in my work I have preferred to deal with connections of this kind indirectly, which is, as I believe, the way of art. Thus it is not the mere undergoing of a terrible or a beautiful experience, neither suffering nor exaltation, which leads to poetry, at least not for me. Only when the experience itself, or more likely no more than some singular aspect or broken small tangent of it, comes somehow to be

deflected or translated into something else, into some myste-
riously larger other thing—which in another day might have
been called the universal or archetypal—does any poem of
mine begin to come into focus. I think of it as a merging of
the personal with the impersonal; the singular commences to
disappear into the plural.

But the exact relations between art and life are not legis-
lated. We know that Dorothy had seen the ten thousand
daffodils, too, but in the poem only William is left wandering
"lonely as a cloud." So also did poor Hugo vanish from the
Potrero Hill evenings of "Bus Stop," though he had been my
faithful companion through many glooms. If he does survive
now, it is only as a generalized ghost, one of

> The quiet lives
> That follow us—
> These lives we lead
> But do not own.

I did sometimes picture him, as the poem goes on to suggest,
standing there, if I should die, puzzled but infinitely patient.
That whole time in San Francisco, as a matter of fact, I went
about, for reasons that scarcely enter the poem, in the grip of
a fear of death. No doubt I did "own" Hugo, if it came to that,
but I did not feel at all in possession of my own life. There
were times when my life felt ghostly to me, and, as in some
special effect contrived for film, I could picture the husk of
my body left behind on a street corner waiting faithfully for
the real self to return. But in writing the poem I was not
tempted to spell out or to make very much out of so slight and
evanescent a feeling, scarcely strong enough to register on the
most sensitive emotional scale. As I concentrate now in an
effort to bring back the time and the place, I see all at once
and for the first time that the buses stopped at the corner
were like a modern equivalent of Charon's ferry, and rain-wet
20th Street a paved-over Styx. The gathering gloom—mist,
drizzle, twilight, fog—would have filled out the infernal impression. It seems obvious, now that I think of it, but even if

so literal a transcription of what the scene suggested had then occurred to me—and it did not, not consciously—I would have kept it out of the poem. It would have been false, too explicit, too histrionic.

The first actual lines—I am sure of it, though I have lost or mislaid the worksheets—began with mention of the lights burning upstairs in unknown rooms. An image with overtones of Weldon Kees, no doubt, and of the very city from which, not quite a decade before, Kees had disappeared; only a block or two along Kansas Street his best friend still lived. I worked at lines meant to evoke the lives of the strangers in those rooms, a motif perhaps retrieved from "Anthony St. Blues," a much earlier poem of mine:

> Withindoors many now enact,
> Behind drawn shades, their shadow lives.

But I was too much absorbed in my own broodings to want to brood long on others; besides, they were very much like us, surely, which was a good part of the poignancy. I had my sense of exile and loneliness, my neurotic fear, my divided self all to find words and figures for, and there, in the very circumstances of daily life, in that extraordinary neighborhood, were facts and details vivid with symbolic presence, only waiting to be mentioned in right relation with one another in order to glow with meaning.

Finding the structure was no problem, as I recall. I had been trying to teach myself to write short free-verse lines; also short syllabic lines. I theorized that there was more control in the short line. A curious problem in syllabics had always interested me and nobody else, apparently, among all the poets—many more then—attracted to that metric. It was the possibility of keeping the number of accents and the number of syllables the same from line to line, but without letting them fall together into the regular foot-patterns, iambs and the like, too often and too familiarly. It's a very technical matter, not awfully important, but it did interest me. Lines in syllabics had usually seemed to go better in odd numbers—

sevens, nines, elevens—since the odd number was a help in avoiding iambics. But now I wanted to try *evens* and, to make it harder on myself, shorter lines than I had attempted or will probably attempt again in syllabics. My sense of syllabics is that as the count gets shorter the line gets harder to compose but, as though in compensation, more "musical," as people like to put it. In "Bus Stop" each line, it will be noticed, has only four syllables. (*Flowers* traditionally may be counted as either one or two syllables; in the line, "Black flowers, black flowers," it counts as one.) Some lines gave me trouble, however easy they may now look, but on the whole they did turn out to be more "musical" than average. The majority are autonomous, more or less end-stopped; they can be heard as lines, which is rare in syllabics. Readers who hear them as accentuals are not wrong to do so, for each line does have two accents. But if these were pure accentual lines no one could expect twenty-four lines in a row to fall by chance into the same syllable count. Because I was keeping this double count, the lines come very close, after all, to being iambic dimeter; yet to those who understand such intricacies, it must be clear that a few lines refuse to submit to the usual iambic conditions (lines 1, 20, and 24).

As for other sound-effects, mostly rhyme or something like it, the thought of calling the poem a song did enter my head, or even of subtitling it "An Urban Song," but a subtitle seemed pretentious. Even so, this was unmistakably a lyric poem, which by its nature could stand quite a lot of *sound*, and I was willing to seek out a fair amount of it, though not very vigorously. I wanted anything which had to do with the sound or "music" to come in very simply and in a completely natural way, almost as though by chance, and chance did, as always in such matters, throw up some coincidences of sound. My intentions in this, being largely impulse and instinct, I was able to carry out more successfully than with the meters. If rhymes showed up—and they did—they were to remain casual, not part of a deliberate scheme, not predictable. Repetition—a type of rhyme itself—turned out to play a larger role in the sound of the poem than the usual rhyming. The rule I set for myself in this was simple and indulgent. I would repeat what-ever I wanted to, anything from a single word to a whole line, and at any time. The effect came to resemble what you get in a poem with multiple refrains, or, more fancifully, when several bells are set swinging at different timings. In the old ballads or in comic songs, not to mention in the master Yeats himself, the meaning of a refrain will seem to shift sometimes with its new context, and I made an effort to imitate that effect. The most obvious case involves repeating "And lives go on." First it is a complete sentence, signifying only that lives continue, persist, endure. But, chiming back in at once, it starts now a longer sentence which before it is done will turn the original meaning into something very different. The lives no longer plod along but are suddenly bright and giving light, beacons. A hopeful note, it seems now, looking back. Yet I was prouder of the more hidden repetition, for those who would notice it, between lines 4 and 23, *hours* echoing *ours.* One of the buried motifs of the poem—that of the displaced self—is here suggested, I would like to think, in the pun on *hours,* but quietly, secretly, perhaps escaping all notice. Read the lines again and see if it is there at all. Perhaps I have imagined it; or has everyone always seen it at once? It only remains to say that whatever the reader is willing to find in *burning* was probably intended, from the simplest turning on of lights to the ardent yearning of the self baffled in loneli-ness. But perhaps not. Only this instant has it occurred to me that at the end St. Augustine may have blundered into yet another Carthage, *burning, burning.*

Certainly the world seemed that year on the point of con-flagration. Goldwater bullies had roamed Nob Hill, our navy was attacked by phantoms in the Tonkin Gulf, Khrushchev fell, China exploded a nuclear device, the first defiant Berke-ley students were dragged roughly down marble staircases, and at Thanksgiving General Taylor took off on his futile fact-finding mission to Vietnam. By late February the official bombing of North Vietnam had begun. The theater company was breaking up, and I fled the city. It sounds dramatic now, but it did feel that way at the time. Not long afterwards, across the continent in Miami, I came upon most of the lines of "Bus Stop" jumbled together on a few pages of the old chemistry notebook I'd found in the Potrero Hill house and, unscrambling them now with ease, finished the poem in an hour or two.

(1983)

Bus Stop

Lights are burning
In quiet rooms
Where lives go on
Resembling ours.

The quiet lives
That follow us—
These lives we lead
But do not own—

Stand in the rain
So quietly
When we are gone,
So quietly . . .

And the last bus
Comes letting dark
Umbrellas out—
Black flowers, black flowers.

And lives go on.
And lives go on
Like sudden lights
At street corners

Or like the lights
In quiet rooms
Left on for hours,
Burning, burning.

Notes on "Variations on Southern Themes"

Variations on Southern Themes

1. At the Cemetery

> But why do I write of the all
> unutterable and the all abysmal? Why
> does my pen not drop from my hand
> on approaching the infinite pity and
> tragedy of all the past? It does, poor
> helpless pen, with what it meets of the
> ineffable, what it meets of the cold
> Medusa-face of life, of all the life
> lived, on every side. Basta, basta!
> —H. James, Notebooks

Above the fence-flowers, like a bloody thumb,
A hummingbird is throbbing, throbbing. Some
Petals take motion now from the beaten wings
In hardly observable obscure quiverings.
And mother stands there, but so still her clothing
Seems to have settled into stone, nothing
To animate her face, nothing to read there—
O plastic rose O clouds O still cedar!
And she stands there a long time while the sky
Ponders her with its great Medusa-eye;
Or in my memory she does.
                                    And then a
Slow blacksnake, lazy with long sunning, glides
Down from its slab, and through the thick grass, and hides
Somewhere among the purpling wild verbena.

2. On the Farm

And I, missing the city intensely at this moment,
Mope and sulk at the window. There's the first owl now,
    quite near,
But the sound hardly registers. And the kerosene lamp
Goes on sputtering, giving off vague medicinal fumes
That make me think of sick-rooms. I have been memorizing
'The Ballad of Reading Gaol,' but the lamplight hurts my
    eyes.
And I am too bored to sleep, restless and bored. I think of
The city . . .
            As, years later, I will recall, without blame,
The tender banalities of those dead Julys—but, ah,
The bitterness of the lampsmoke then, the pure aloneness!
And now I yawn, and the old dream of being a changeling
Returns. I hear the owl, and I think myself like that owl—
Proud, almost unnoticed—or like some hero in Homer
Protected by a cloud let down by the gods to save me.

3. In the Train, Heading North through Florida, Late at Night and Long Ago, and Ending with a Line from Thomas Wolfe

Midnight or after, and the little lights
Glitter like lost beads from a broken necklace
Beyond smudged windows, lost and irretrievable—
Some promise of romance these Southern nights
Never entirely keep—unless, sleepless,
We should pass down dim corridors again
To stand, braced in a swaying vestibule,
Alone with the darkness and the wind—out there
Nothing but pines and one new road perhaps,
Straight and white, aimed at the distant gulf—
And hear, from the smoking-room, the sudden high-pitched
Whinny of laughter pass from throat to throat;
And the great wheels smash and pound beneath our feet.

It is true that there was a brief period, three or four years perhaps, when I thought of myself as a Southern writer. My first short story was anthologized in an O. Henry annual, and I was so carried away by the chance to make up a contributor's note that I found myself claiming to be "of the South" and with "no desire to leave it." The spell of Faulkner's wild and steamy prose was upon me in those days, and of the innocent fairy-tale world Eudora Welty's early stories conjured up. What they wrote seemed larger than life to me, an art of wonderful exaggerations and fantastications, a kind of dreaming; only dimly could anything like the South I had been born and brought up in be discerned beneath the mythic trappings. The ideas which gave me some purchase on this South, so much grander than my own, had come by way of the Fugitive-Agrarians. I wrote a master's thesis on their work, and for a while the sentimental ironies of their poetry imposed upon my own experience a set of attitudes which were not destined to survive.

A spoiled heroic figure like Faulkner's Sutpen had always been nearly as remote from my world, my desires and opinions, as Odysseus himself, and it should not have taken the hardening of Southern attitudes in the fifties—a reaction to the Supreme Court school decision—to drive home that realization finally. In poems of the time—"Beyond the Hunting Woods" and "Southern Gothic" in particular—I paid my respectful farewells to the symbols of the Old South, which seemed by then far more literary than lived. The decaying houses in those early poems represented the emptiness and hollowness I had come to find in such idealizations of the South, mixed, no doubt, with a certain lingering affection.

Driving through Virginia in the late summer of 1980, after many years spent outside the South, I noticed that we were passing tree after tree with large caterpillar tents hanging down from their branches. It was a slowed-down, drawn-out moment of recognition. That was how, when I was a child, my grandfather's modest grove of pecan trees had looked, infested and festooned with just such gauzy sacs. I could remember my grandfather standing on the porch of his house in Boston, Georgia, towering above me as he gestured out at sunset towards the ruined trees. Now I saw again *cocoons of caterpillars in pecans.*

Here was an interesting texture of sounds, crisscrossing but patternless. Words sometimes, through likeness of sound, become bound to one another by ties remotely like those of human kinship. This is not to propose that any *meaning* attaches to the sounds independent of the words. But the interlocking sounds do seem to reinforce and in some curious way to authenticate the meanings of the words, perhaps indirectly to deepen and enlarge them. A part of the very nature of poetry lies in this fact.

Nor was it an accident that this run of sounds had fallen out into an iambic pentameter. I have a temperament much tempted by difficulty and proscription, which probably harks back to childhood. No act had ever seemed quite so pure and challenging in those days as the one forbidden by authority. And lately, against the better judgment of practically everybody, I had been thinking of writing sonnets again, after a lapse of twenty years. The reputation of the sonnet for backwardness matched the reputation of the very region before me, which only recently had begun to come out from under its dark historic cloud. If public sentiment ruled against the sonnet and its pentameters, that was enough to draw me on. Already out of this one line many lines could be imagined flowing, many sonnets, an entire sequence, exploring and plumbing my sense of the South, whatever that might prove to be once I began work.

On the Porch

There used to be a way the sunlight caught
The cocoons of caterpillars in the pecans.
The boy's shadow would lengthen to a man's
Across the yard then, slowly. And if he thought
Some sleepy god had dreamed it all up—well,
There stood the grandfather, Lincoln-tall and solemn,
Tapping his pipe out on the white-flaked column,
Carefully, carefully, as though it were his job.
And they would watch the pipe-stars as they fell.
As for the quiet, the same train always broke it.
Then the great silver watch rose from its pocket

For them to check the hour, the dark fob
Dangling the watch between them like a moon.
It would be evening soon then, very soon.

But was this grandfather not less godlike than the actual one
remembered had in life been? And this effort to translate the
mundane—pipe sparks and pocket watch—into the astro-
nomical and cosmic seemed doomed to extravagance and sentimentality. Whatever sense of awe, whatever sense of en-
countering and being accepted into a world of mythic
proportions might be present, was there it seemed only by
force of will and desire.

There is always a drawer reserved for these disappoint-
ments. With this one so painstakingly worked out, however, a
clearer picture of what the other sonnets might be had begun
to appear, not that in the event it would prove altogether
accurate. In each, some half-archetypal or symbolic figure
would be placed against a classic background or scene, this to
be realized in exact and personal detail rescued from memory.
The freaks and fantastics of recent Southern literature were to
be shunned, the rhetoric of past glories choked off. If this
meant sacrificing much by which the Southern in literature
had come to be identified, the poems might claim to be no less
true for all of that.

In my mind was a picture of my mother standing motionless in
bright sunlight beside the family plot in the cemetery in
Boston, Georgia. But was she weeping, or praying, or involved
in something yet more hidden and mysterious? And did this
picture come from memory or was it purely imaginary?

In any case, it has always struck me as a very pretty cemetery, a sort of fallen and faded Eden. The snake, last sighted
in actual fact on a sunning-stone in some Carolina stream,
hundreds of miles distant, was not to intrude upon this Eden
until the last few lines. And the verbena *was* in bloom when
last checked on, high and flourishing enough to harbor a busy
invisible life. A mower at work downslope remained quietly
and stubbornly in the text for weeks, rhyming with one thing
after another. Otherwise the stillness was almost absolute, al-

most pure. The hummingbird showed its minute flash of red, and I wrote for line 8: *The ruby wing, or the stray clouds, or the cedar.* But a student of mine, something of a naturalist, told me that no American hummingbird possessed such a wing color, and the family bird book confirmed my error. What had I really seen? Better to change the line. The very first version of this crucial line, incidentally, had been jotted down during a visit to the cemetery many months before, antedating even the *cocoons* line, but without any place then for it to fit: *Cedar and mockingbird and plastic rose.* It has proved an extremely hard line to get right and to find a place for.

At some point I had copied out from Henry James' notebooks into a notebook of my own James' question concerning "the all abysmal," stopping with that phrase. (James was recalling a visit of his own to a cemetery in Cambridge, just across the river, coincidentally, from the Boston of the North.) It took the poet Henri Coulette to remind me of the sentences with which the James entry so movingly continues. Thus emerged the Medusa image.

Meanwhile I had begun to simplify the sonnet form, for convenience and novelty both. The usual crossing rhymes came down to a plainer stream of couplets, with the single exception of the rhyming pair connecting line 11 and line 14, a token nod to what might have been; and several of the rhymes were left—or made—purposely barbaric, as if to suggest the awkwardness of truth or some disdain for the artful. In the end I found myself somewhat regretfully abandoning the historical past tense and the more generic third person out of which the poems had come. The voicing seemed better that way, as when a song is transposed to a key more conformable to the singer's voice.

Some of the discomforts felt in childhood on my other grandfather's farm, just east of Tifton, Georgia, had come up in earlier poems (in "First Death," for instance). I could understand those feelings now as signs of alienation. One vivid memory was of sitting all afternoon in the sweltering front bedroom of that farmhouse at about age twelve or thirteen, alone, while everybody else seemed to be out working in the fields or off in the kitchen. I was reading a pocketbook anthology of poetry which happened to contain "The Ballad of Reading Gaol." I felt shut up in a sort of prison myself, filled with nameless small guilts and large longings. The attempt to memorize was bound to fail—I could never memorize—but it was the sign of some wish to establish my uniqueness, my difference. I felt isolated but superior, a prince in exile. Also safe. The feeling was one of rich complications and balances.

The normal pentameter of the sonnet is stretched out in "On the Farm" to a very long syllabic line having a strict count of fourteen. The first line itself, which had the sort of rhythmic run I wanted, became the model for this. Prose I was determined to avoid, and yet the very long line does pull towards prose. Most long lines having a fine speaking sound make use of pauses, often at a sort of balancing point near the middle of the line, but with a certain amount of interesting shifting about. (I had tried something like this before in a poem called "Mule Team and Poster.") A generous distribution of such pauses seems to be almost enough to keep the lines rhythmically alive and breathing. Along with the general pull towards prose, all rhymes soon dropped out, though by no means all interest in sound. These relaxed syllabics should stand out distinctly against the pentameters of the other poems, and vice versa.

As for "In the Train," the larger-than-life figure, not very specifically outlined, is a sort of Wolfean Telemachus, the adolescent romantic wanderer. But it is really the emotion, the welling up and crystallization of the ecstasy of travel, that grows to large proportion here. Since my own adolescence the images of Thomas Wolfe's night train journey had haunted me—a young man's author, if he is anything—and before finishing this poem I must have turned over, for the first time in decades, hundreds of his pages, making notes. Evidence of an aspiration towards sonnethood remains in the rhymes of lines 1 and 4. The writing was tuned up to as high a romantic pitch as anything I had done in years, somewhere up along the scale towards Wolfe himself, it may be. The climax, saved back as long as it could be, came with line 13—Wolfe's, with the tense altered—at which point the "sonnet" stops abruptly, one line short. But this sudden halt goes along with my conviction that poems ought to stop when they are done, and after the Wolfean apotheosis there was nothing more to be done or said. Using *we*, I was joined again by my dead friend Robert Vaughn, the most profound romantic anyone can ever have wished to know, to whom at one stage the poem was tentatively dedicated. The two of us were, as it happens, on our way to nowhere more legendary than Manhattan. But Manhattan would do, for wonders and splendors; in fact, it did do.

This whole set of variations, however long it may finally prove to be, can only aim to be transparent. The chief problem for a critic might well be this very lack of difficulty, for I have observed that critics prefer to untie trickier knots. Yet history, biography, literature all do surround and underlie the sequence. In the absence of photographs from the family album, various picture books having the South as subject, such as Eudora Welty's, might fill in some of the background. Photographs from the Farm Security Administration of the thirties would be the right period, more or less, and have the right look. Many of them call back the sad beauty of the time and place.

Although they are obviously not sonnets such as could have been written in 1590 or 1820 or even 1950, the poems are no less obviously traditional. The lines *are* lines, with an integrity of their own, unlike most lines now being written. The meters have affected not just the composition and expressiveness of the poems but, for better or worse, can be seen as part of their very body and substance. For better, I would hope; inevitably and inextricably, in any case.

Political metaphors as applied to literary history can be objectionable as well as hackneyed, but they are convenient. In such terms these variations can be called radically conservative, I believe, if we agree that this refers to an esthetic position only and has absolutely nothing to do with politics. For one thing, meters now are taken to be the party badge of the conservative, and automatically so, by readers—often enough by poets themselves—who have very little understanding of how they work. The idea that art may possess an order and that life might be illuminated by that—even so basic and classical an idea as this—is considered unnatural, insincere, no longer up-to-date or relevant. But this looks like one of those moments when the most radical position of all—certainly the minority position, the position of the outsider—would be one that sought to carry on or to reconnect somehow with tradition. I think of the memorizers of forbidden books in the old Ray Bradbury fantasy, members of an underground. By tradition I do not of course mean Milton and Wordsworth only, but Hardy and Frost, Williams and Stevens, Baudelaire and Rimbaud, etc. The age of experiment is exhausted and moribund, temporarily at least. There is no one with the brilliance and authority of Williams, and the whole lineage that came after him seems to be wearing thin, like soil needing rotation. Meanwhile, much of American poetry is awash in a great ruck and welter of sentimentality. In most universities, most journals, the attitudes prevailing are attitudes left over from the sixties; but the sixties are dead. Let us consider instead the twenties and thirties: Brecht and Alberti, perhaps. Not Trakl or Rilke any longer now, however exalted or evocative, but rather the social realism and hard, definite outlines of Brecht. Not Neruda or Vallejo any longer now, however passionate and sincere, but rather the cooler technical brilliancies, the mysterious precisions of Alberti. A tradition could be put back together starting with not much more than this. Not forgetting rhythm; not forgetting truth.

(1983)

UNDER DISCUSSION
Donald Hall, General Editor

Volumes in the Under Discussion series collect reviews and essays about individual poets. The series is concerned with contemporary American and English poets about whom the consensus has not yet been formed and the final vote has not been taken. Titles in the series include:

Elizabeth Bishop and Her Art
  edited by Lloyd Schwartz and Sybil P. Estess
Richard Wilbur's Creation *edited and with an*
  Introduction by Wendy Salinger
Reading Adrienne Rich *edited by Jane Roberta Cooper*

Forthcoming volumes will examine the work of Robert Bly and Allen Ginsberg, among others.

Please write for further information on available editions and current prices.

Ann Arbor   **The University of Michigan Press**